LOW FAT
For Life
COOKBOOK

LOW FAT
For Life
COOKBOOK

SUE KREITZMAN

Photography by Ian O'Leary

Food styling by Janice Murfitt

The Reader's Digest Association (Canada) Ltd.

MONTREAL

A DK PUBLISHING BOOK

Art Editor Sue Storey

Editor Janice Anderson

Assistant Editor Lorraine Turner

DTP Designer Bridget Roseberry

Managing Editor Mary Ling

Deputy Art Director Carole Ash

Production Manager Maryann Rogers

Production Controller Manjit Sihra

North American Editors Iris Rosoff, Joan Whitman

For Freda

Published in Canada in 1998 by
The Reader's Digest Association (Canada) Ltd.
215 Redfern Avenue, Westmount, Quebec, H3Z 2V9

For information on this and other Reader's Digest products or to request a
catalogue, please call our 24-hour Customer Service hotline at 1-800-465-0780

You can also visit us on the World Wide Web at
http://www.readersdigest.ca

First published in Great Britain in 1998 by Dorling Kindersley Limited,
9 Henrietta Street, London WC2E 8PS

Canadian Cataloguing in Publication Data
Kreitzman, Sue
Low fat for life cookbook

ISBN 0-88850-621-X

1. Low-fat diet–Recipes. I. Title.
RM237.7.K745 1998   641.5'638   C98-900327-2

READER'S DIGEST and the Pegasus logo are registered trademarks of
The Reader's Digest Association, Inc.

Reproduced in Singapore by Colourscan
Printed and bound in Great Britain by Butler & Tanner Ltd
98 99 00 01/5 4 3 2 1

CONTENTS

INTRODUCTION 6

GALLERY OF LOW-FAT DISHES 10

*A mouthwatering array of dishes for all
kinds of meals, rich in color, bursting with
flavor, and amazingly low in fat*

INTRODUCTION

HOW I LOVE FOOD! Vivid color, interesting textures, bombastic flavor, and lots of pizzazz – I want it all. My expertise centers on low-fat cooking, the result of an almost lifetime battle with obesity coupled with my enduring passion for food in all its glorious and fascinating aspects. My philosophy is no added fat – I don't believe in substituting one high-fat regime for another – and my aim is to help you achieve a total low-fat, high nutrition gastronomic lifestyle.

I'm not the food police, however; you must come to a health-giving, low-fat way on your own. An enforced, unimaginative spell of low-fat eating against one's will means cottage cheese, naked slabs of steamed fish and grilled chicken breasts, piles of raw vegetables and undressed salads, and no desserts at all. The result? Dreadful boredom often followed by a desperate urge to binge.

MAKING A LOW-FAT LIFESTYLE ENJOYABLE

Nutrition without sensual enjoyment is grim indeed. Healthy eating must be a celebration, not a punishment. You will not find a lengthy, scientifically based explanation of fats here: all you need to know about fats and the place of cholesterol in the diet is in Fat Facts (see pages 162–3).

Successful low-fat cooking depends on technique. That is why this book emphasizes technique above all, not just in the Techniques sections (see pages 28–37), but throughout the recipe sections. I want you to be able to apply these techniques generally to all your cooking, not just to the specific recipes I have chosen for this book.

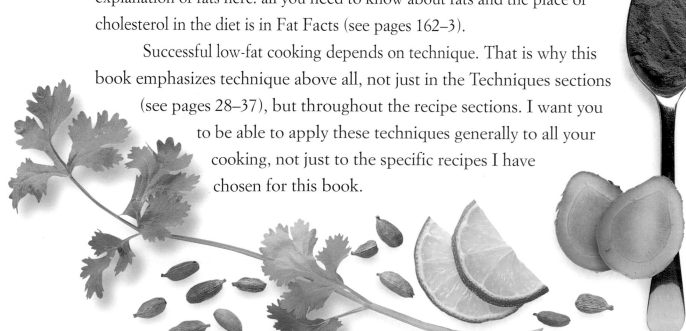

If you take on board the oil-water spray, the stock sauté, the flavor infusions, the sauces made from vegetable purees, and so on, a low-fat kitchen lifestyle becomes easy and natural. Above all, your meals will be a pleasurable, well-rounded fiesta of vegetables, fruits, grains, fish, and lean meat and poultry, with the emphasis on vegetables, fruits, and grains. You will find lots of sauces, salsas, garnishes, and embellishments made from vegetables and fruits. They add color, excitement, and plenty of wonderful nutrition. I always want my recipes to resonate with big, round, intense flavors and fragrances. The lack of added fat means that the cloying, blunting quality of those fats (and oils) is gone.

THE INTELLIGENT OPTION?

There are many reasons for embracing a low-fat way of life. It is an intelligent, healthy, and fulfilling method of weight control and weight maintenance, of course, but it goes far beyond that. Low dietary fat levels are a necessity for those who suffer from assorted medical problems – heart and artery disease, high blood cholesterol levels, diabetes, and gall bladder problems, among them – but they have also become a lifetime food regime of choice for those enlightened people who want a healthier, thoroughly modern, lighter way of eating.

Now that we are nearly at the end of the twentieth century, heavy, fat-based, greasy, and cloying food seems hopelessly outdated. Those who want a fresh vibrancy to their meals, who want to dine well yet not end a meal feeling stuffed, bloated, and weighed down, and who want to prevent later problems with obesity and fat-related diseases, turn to lowered fat levels with great relief and enthusiasm. Suddenly, those reactionary chefs and foodies who continue to cling tenaciously to their old, fat-based techniques seem sadly obsolete and misguided. So enjoy the present, and look forward to a healthy and gastronomically rewarding future. Revel in the goodness of a low-fat, full-flavor lifestyle, easily achieved when you follow my basic cooking techniques and use (and adapt to your own tastes) the recipes here.

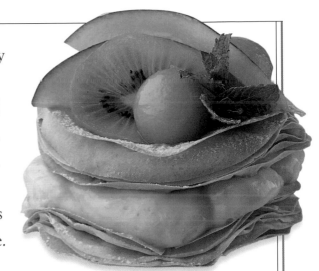

NUTRITIONAL ANALYSIS

Some recipes in this book are extremely low in fat, some are reduced fat. A sensible low-fat diet will derive approximately 20–25 percent of total calories from fat. That works out to about 50 grams of fat per day. All recipes have a nutritional analysis giving an idea of what the fat levels actually are, but remember:

The analyses accompanying the recipes are only approximate. Nutrient levels in food can vary from time to time and from place to place, and are not standard.

Sometimes, the figures for saturated and unsaturated fats do not equal the total fat figure. This is because the fat total includes other non-fatty acid materials as well as fatty acids.

The symbol "<1g" in the analyses means the recipe quantity analyzed contains less than 1 gram of the fat named. "Neg" ("negligible") means 0.1g or 0.2g of fat.

There is no need to turn mealtimes into grim accounting sessions. Use my techniques wherever possible, and cut out high-fat foods and added fats from your meals, and your fat levels will fall very neatly into place.

COOKING NOTES

1 All recipes are written in imperial and metric measurements. Use one or the other, but do not mix measurements.

2 Teaspoons and tablespoons are level: 1tsp = 5ml, 1tbsp = 15ml. Eggs, when used (which is not often), are large.

3 Appetites and food "shapes" vary, so take the portion sizes as a general suggestion and adjust to your needs.

4 Because ovens vary greatly, oven timings given in recipes can only be approximate. Always preheat the oven. For convection ovens, reduce the oven temperature by about 20°F (see the manufacturer's instructions for your oven).

GALLERY
_of_
LOW-FAT
DISHES

THE RICHLY COLORFUL PHOTOGRAPHS ON THESE

PAGES SHOW HOW GORGEOUS LOW-FAT FOOD CAN LOOK.

OF COURSE, TO FIND OUT JUST HOW GREAT IT

CAN TASTE, YOU MUST MAKE THE RECIPES FOR YOURSELF.

THERE IS PLENTY OF CHOICE: PAGES OF POULTRY

AND FISH DISHES, TORTILLA FILLINGS, PIZZAS AND PASTA

DISHES, OFFERING ALL THE AUTHENTIC FLAVORS OF

TRADITIONAL VERSIONS PLUS MANY EXCITING NEW IDEAS

FOR TOPPINGS AND SAUCES. AND THERE ARE DREAMY

DESSERTS, WHERE LAYERS OF FRUIT MINGLE ENTICINGLY

WITH DELICATELY FLAVORED CREAM TOPPINGS.

PIZZAS

Opposite:
TOMATO &
MOZZARELLA
(See page 145)

Per serving	Low fat	Full fat
Total fat (g)	5	30
Calories	361	591

GOOEY MELTED CHEESE, tender cloves of pan-braised garlic, garden-fresh herbs, earthy wild mushrooms, silky sautéed peppers, olive- and chili-flecked tomato sauce, juicy tomatoes bursting with flavor, all piled onto a crisp, freshly baked yeast dough, make irresistible party fare for family and friends.

"Food … lovingly prepared, and eaten in good company, warms the being with something more than mere intake of calories."

Marjorie Kinnan Rawlings,
Cross Creek Cookery

PEPPERS & FETA CHEESE
(See page 145)

Per serving	Low fat	Full fat
Total fat (g)	7	32
Calories	418	641

MUSHROOM & PESTO
(See page 145)

Per serving	Low fat	Full fat
Total fat (g)	21	58
Calories	558	895

For ultimate pizza pizzazz generously mix your favorite ingredients using tantalizing textures, flavors, and colors

SAUSAGE & CREAMY
SPINACH *(See page 145)*

Per serving	Low fat	Full fat
Total fat (g)	18	89
Calories	545	1185

TOMATO & RED ONION
(See page 145)

Per serving	Low fat	Full fat
Total fat (g)	9	44
Calories	415	765

LAYERED DESSERTS

Opposite:
FRUIT
CREPES
(See page 121)

Per serving	Low fat	Full fat
Total fat (g)	neg	13
Calories	255	325

TAKE NATURE'S GLORIOUS BOUNTY of fruit, add creamy clouds of whipped ricotta, perhaps a dusting of cocoa or a splash or two of intensely fragrant liqueurs, and you have a delicious selection of outrageously rich yet low-fat desserts. They are guaranteed to tempt the taste buds and do no damage to the waistline.

"There is something skewed about an eating regime designed ... for every part of your body except the tip of your tongue."

Ellen Goodman,
Boston Globe

MERINGUE STACK
(See page 135)

Per serving	Low fat	Full fat
Total fat (g)	5	40
Calories	184	477

MANGO MILLEFEUILLE
(See page 136)

Per serving	Low fat	Full fat
Total fat (g)	11	36
Calories	274	590

Heavenly light-as-air layers, with fruits and creamy fillings, form seductive desserts for special occasions

CHOCOLATE CREPES
(See page 121)

Per serving	Low fat	Full fat
Total fat (g)	9	77
Calories	366	886

PASTA

Opposite:
OPEN
RAVIOLI
(See page 108)

Per serving	Low fat	Full fat
Total fat (g)	4g	45
Calories	358	726

TAKE A GENEROUS AMOUNT OF A RICH SAUCE full of colorful and nutritious vegetables. Add it to your favorite pasta, with a creamy sauce based on low-fat cheeses, if you like. Sprinkle with plenty of chopped fresh herbs. It all adds up to a dazzling collection of highly satisfying and amazingly low-fat meals.

"Italians do not regard food as merely fuel. They regard it as medicine for the soul..."

Barbara Grizzuti Harrison,
Italian Days (1989)

LASAGNA
(See page 111)

Per serving	Low fat	Full fat
Total fat (g)	12	61
Calories	346	834

FARFALLE WITH PEA
PUREE & PEPPERS
(See page 108)

Per serving	Low fat	Full fat
Total fat (g)	4	23
Calories	462	633

CONCHIGLIONI WITH
BROCCOLI PESTO
(See page 111)

Per serving	Low fat	Full fat
Total fat (g)	9	21
Calories	356	461

For perfect pasta partnerships, mix zingy vegetable toppings, creamy sauces, and your favorite pasta shape

SAUCES & SALSAS

Opposite: VEGETABLE & DUCK *(See pages 52, 65 & 90)*

Per serving	Low fat	Full fat
Total fat (g)	5	39
Calories	160	446

SAUCES AND SALSAS, made from a wide selection of vegetables, fruits, and herbs, bring low-fat food to vivid, exuberant life. Anyone who thinks that a low-fat lifestyle equals boredom and austerity just hasn't experienced the full potential of this wonderful food. Who could be bored in the face of such glory?

"You will find salsa on Mexican tables at any time. It is ... refreshing served just with tortillas."

Diana Kennedy, *The Cuisines of Mexico (1982)*

SAUSAGE & ROASTED VEGETABLE SALSA
(See pages 65 & 94)

Per serving	Low fat	Full fat
Total fat (g)	5	22
Calories	450	596

MUSHROOMS MADE WILD
(See page 74)

Per serving	Low fat	Full fat
Total fat (g)	2	9
Calories	102	164

CHICKEN WITH SWEET POTATO & LIME
(See page 88)

Per serving	Low fat	Full fat
Total fat (g)	2	19
Calories	207	336

Spilling lavishly from tortilla cones, sauces and salsas delight the senses with color and fragrance

FISH

Opposite:
TUNA WITH
LEMON &
GARLIC
(See page 102)

Per serving	Low fat	Full fat
Total fat (g)	7	71
Calories	265	835

FISH IS THE ULTIMATE HEALTH FOOD, and the ultimate fast food as well. And it is surely the most elegant of ingredients. Cook it quickly, sauce it wisely, and serve with pride. Overcooking, and adding sauces that swamp rather than complement the delicate flavor of the fish, would ruin the whole effect.

"Fish dinners will make a man spring like a flea."

Thomas Jordan,
(1640)

SALMON WITH
YELLOW PEPPER &
TARRAGON SAUCE
(See page 104)

Per serving	Low fat	Full fat
Total fat (g)	20	61
Calories	505	873

HALIBUT WITH
TOMATO & EGGPLANT
(See page 104)

Per serving	Low fat	Full fat
Total fat (g)	6	53
Calories	378	802

ROASTED MONKFISH
WITH GARLIC SAUCE
(See page 103)

Per serving	Low fat	Full fat
Total fat (g)	2	44
Calories	156	536

Why long for Béarnaise? Pureed yellow peppers and a tarragon infusion impart similar luxury to succulent salmon

CREAMY DESSERTS

Opposite:
FRUIT
RICOTTA
TIRAMISU
(See page 127)

Per serving	Low fat	Full fat
Total fat (g)	12	45
Calories	344	651

A LOVELY, LIGHT SOFTNESS characterizes low-fat replacements for cream, such as ricotta, Quark, and fromage frais, ensuring that desserts made with them are luxuriously smooth, but never cloying. Intensely fruity preserves, citrus-sharp marmalades, and richly dark cocoa powder provide depth of flavor.

"A...hostess excited a solemn children's party to ecstasy by the...words 'Now, let's start with the strawberries and cream.'"
Molly Keane,
Nursery Cooking (1985)

Light-as-air mousses and rich, creamy desserts make delicious finales to any meal

BLUEBERRY COMPOTE
WITH CREAM TOPPING
(See pages 130 & 137)

Per serving	Low fat	Full fat
Total fat (g)	7	45
Calories	191	480

CHOCOLATE
CHEESECAKE MOUSSE
(See page 122)

Per serving	Low fat	Full fat
Total fat (g)	12	60
Calories	277	697

PEACH COMPOTE
WITH CREAM TOPPING
(See pages 130 & 137)

Per serving	Low fat	Full fat
Total fat (g)	7	45
Calories	232	519

POULTRY

Opposite: DUCK
BREAST &
CRANBERRY
CHUTNEY
(See page 89)

Per serving	Low fat	Full fat
Total fat (g)	6	62
Calories	241	700

TAKE MOUTH-TINGLING MARINADES, the choice of the glorious spices of Asia, and the pick of the world's marvelous production of fruits, vegetables, and herbs. Add them to delicately flavored chicken and more robust duck. The result is an unrivaled selection of low-fat poultry dishes for memorable feasting.

"There is no way of preparing a chicken which I don't like."

Marcella Hazan,
Marcella's Kitchen (1987)

CHICKEN WITH SWEET POTATO & LIME
(See page 88)

Per serving	Low fat	Full fat
Total fat (g)	2	34
Calories	260	519

CHICKEN BREAST WITH BRAISED PRUNES
(See page 87)

Per serving	Low fat	Full fat
Total fat (g)	2	40
Calories	178	500

CHICKEN TANDOORI
(See page 86)

Per serving	Low fat	Full fat
Total fat (g)	3	9
Calories	170	239

Zesty marinades; vegetables, herbs, and fruits; imaginative seasonings. Use lavishly with poultry for fine flavors

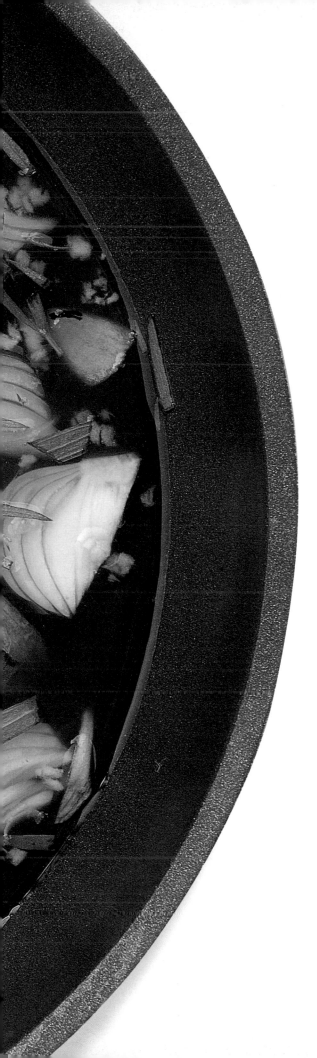

LOW-FAT ESSENTIALS

Successful low-fat cooking depends on good, fresh ingredients carefully prepared and cleverly used and combined with no added fats or very high-fat foods. This section describes food preparation and other techniques that drastically reduce the fat needed in cooking while ensuring that flavor remains high. There are also detailed notes on the wide range of ingredients available to the low-fat cook, and a survey of the kinds of pans, cookware, and utensils that help make low-fat cooking easy and enjoyable.

TECHNIQUES

TRADITIONAL CUISINES ARE BASED ON FAT because, for centuries, people needed a great deal of fat for survival. Fat, calorie-dense foods were vital for warmth, energy, and for making stored fat for lean times ahead. Today, technology and an ample food supply have drastically decreased our need for fat calories, yet the culinary arts and sciences have stayed in the past. Recipes still insist on the need to sauté in butter, fry in oils and lard, enrich with cream, and cover with high-fat cheeses.

I believe that it is not enough simply to cut back on fat. To cook our way into the next century, we need to adopt a whole new set of techniques. We will never eliminate fat altogether, nor should we try. We need a small quantity of essential fatty acids each day, and we need the fat-soluble vitamins found in fatty substances. A good variety of vegetables, fruits, whole grains, fish, lean meat, and poultry, plus occasional vitamin-fortified foods (cereals and skim milk powder, for instance) supply the body's needs.

On the following pages I tell you about the techniques I have developed for taking cooking into a new, low-fat age. First are some techniques to drastically reduce the amount of fat in foodstuffs and recipes. These include oil-water sprays; using stock-sautés instead of the oil, butter, and other fats of basic sautéing; and replacing sauces and toppings based on a butter and flour roux, eggs, and milk or cream with sauces based on low-fat and no-fat dairy products, vegetable purees, and concentrated fat-free stocks. And there is the practical matter of cutting all visible fat off meats and removing all the skin and fat from poultry.

Second come ways of adding intensified flavor to dishes without fat. Here my flavor infusion techniques are essential.

Third are techniques based on using vegetables, particularly peppers, garlic, and eggplant, as replacements for a proportion of the higher-fat ingredients in dishes and for adding texture, color, and flavor. Finally, we need to be technologically savvy, taking advantage of all the research that has gone into the production of nonstick cooking utensils.

OIL-WATER SPRAYS
see page 29

FLAVOR INFUSIONS
see pages 32–3

LOW-FAT INGREDIENTS
see pages 40–3

COOKING EQUIPMENT
see pages 38–9

REDUCING FAT IN COOKING

THE SECRETS OF DELICIOUS, rich-tasting, low-fat cooking lie in this handful of basic trustworthy techniques. They allow you to keep fat down and flavor up. The oil-water spray is particularly handy: it delivers far less oil than commercial oil sprays, and the quality of oil – since you choose it yourself – is high. A spritz of olive, safflower, or sunflower oil is perfect for roasting or broiling, or try walnut or sesame oil with salads and Asian dishes. The stock sauté paired with flavor infusions forms another extremely useful technique. Apply these tricks to all your cooking, not just to the recipes here.

OIL-WATER SPRAY

For low-fat cooking, frying, even shallow-frying, is out. An oil-water spray allows successful grill-frying or oven-frying. Fill a new, clean plant mister or small plastic spray bottle with seven eighths water and one eighth oil. Give the bottle a good shake before using it to spray food or broilers, pots, and pans. Keep separate bottles for olive oil (for a richer flavor), sunflower oil (for all-purpose use), walnut oil (for a lovely fragrance), and sesame oil (to garnish Asian dishes).

OIL-WATER SPRAY   OLIVE OIL   SUNFLOWER OIL   WALNUT OIL   SESAME OIL

USING THE OIL-WATER SPRAY

1 A light spritz with the oil-water spray gives a sufficient coating on grills and broiler pans that lets you broil and grill-fry fish, meat cutlets, and chicken pieces with great success. For oven-frying, use a sturdy, nonstick baking sheet.

2 An oil-water spray lets food for broiling, grill-frying, or oven-frying be given the lightest possible coating of oil to stop the food drying out or sticking to the pan or baking sheet. Brushing oil on food before broiling becomes a thing of the past.

BASIC SAUTEING WITHOUT FATS

Without butter, oil, or margarine, how does one manage the basic sauté that begins most savory recipes? Simple: substitute stock or stock and wine for the fat or oil. Make your own fat-free stock (chicken, vegetable, or fish, depending on the recipe), eliminating any initial oil sautéing of conventional stock-making, or buy jars of concentrated stocks now sold by many supermarkets. Mushroom soaking liquid makes a flavor-rich stock (see right). Fresh mushrooms sautéed in stock, wine, and teriyaki sauce rather than oil (120 calories per tablespoon!) have a superb and intense flavor. Another good source of very low-fat stock is Swiss bouillon powder, available in health food stores. Do not use bouillon cubes, which have a high fat content and which tend to be salty.

MUSHROOM SOAKING LIQUID is a superb stock. Soak dried mushrooms (such as porcini) in plenty of very hot water for 30 minutes. Strain to remove grit. Use both rehydrated mushrooms and the liquid in cooking. Freeze extra stock for later use.

VEGETABLE, CHICKEN, AND FISH STOCK can be made without any initial sautéing in oil. The first two can be used in most recipes here; keep fish stock for fish recipes. Strain chicken stock well and chill for several hours before scraping off all fat.

SAUTEING DELICATE FOODS like shrimp without fat is easy and flavorful when stock and wine, citrus juice, or aromatic sauces replace the oil. Flavor infusion ingredients intensify the whole dish. The Cajun Prawns (*left*, and see page 100) are cooked in a flavor infusion reduced twice to intensify the flavor. Vegetable or chicken stock, lemon juice, and Worcestershire sauce are used for the first reduction; fish stock is poured in for the second reduction.

Two stocks, lemon juice, and an aromatic sauce are the liquids in this flavor infusion.

LOW-FAT SAUCES & TOPPINGS

White sauces made with a butter and flour roux (or oil and flour in some parts of the world) and whole milk and/or cream have no place in a modern low-fat lifestyle. Butter–egg yolk emulsion sauces are passé as well, along with beurre blanc and sauces that call for the boiling down of gallons of cream. But wonderful full-bodied sauces can be made with vegetable purees: tomatoes, peppers, eggplant, roasted or braised garlic, even peas. Creamy sauces are also possible given the wealth of no-fat, low-fat, and medium-fat dairy products available. Particularly successful as a rich topping is a custard of ricotta, egg whites, and Parmesan (*below*).

Grilled Vegetable Lasagna (see page 110) with a rich, creamy, yet very low-fat topping.

1 To make the low-fat topping, Ricotta Parmesan Custard (see page 80), first beat egg whites and ricotta cheese together.

2 Add skim milk and grated Parmesan for a rich, creamy topping for lasagnas, gratins, and similar dishes.

STABILIZING YOGURT

Very low-fat yogurt is thin and watery, and curdles (separates) if you try to cook with it. Make it thick and creamy by straining it in a cheesecloth-lined sieve. Stabilize it for savory cooking by whisking in Dijon mustard (about a teaspoonful to 10oz/300g) before adding it to a dish during cooking.

REMOVING FAT FROM MEAT & POULTRY

I believe that the occasional serving of lean meat is an important component of a well-rounded diet. Remember that even the leanest cuts of meat, although they may have relatively sparse fat marbling, have surrounding fat that must be trimmed away. Pork tenderloin and pork loin steaks are real standbys, ideal for roasting, pan-braising, and broiling, and even for grinding for lean sausages (augmented with roasted eggplant – see page 37). Trim the meat well first, with scissors or a sharp knife. Poultry should be trimmed very well, too. In most cases, the fat-laden skin strips away easily, leaving just scraps of skin and fat to be trimmed off.

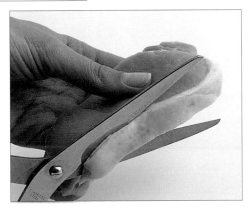

PORK CHOPS are easily trimmed of their rim of fat, especially if you use kitchen scissors, which are easier and more efficient than a sharp knife.

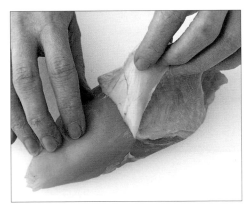

CHICKEN BREASTS are also easily skinned – simply get a good grip on one edge of the skin and pull, then use scissors or a knife to trim off all traces of skin and fat.

FLAVOR INFUSIONS

FLAVOR INFUSIONS MADE BY COOKING DOWN good stock and wine with a selection of well-chosen flavor components replace the oil- and butter-based sautés of conventional cooking. The infusion ensures that the finished dish resonates with round, intense, and well-balanced flavor. As in most conventional sautés, a flavor infusion for low-fat cooking begins with onions and garlic, then other ingredients are added, according to the nature of the particular recipe. Illustrated on this page are the main groups of ingredients that are used in various combinations to give flavor infusions their individual intensity.

BASIC INGREDIENTS

These groups are not definitive: cook's preferences and what is in the kitchen pantry will suggest alternatives.

SPICES *(below) give flavor and color to infusions. When simmered in stock and wine, they become gentle and mellow, and all their flavor is released to mingle with other tastes.*

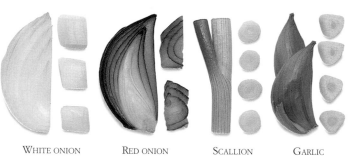

WHITE ONION   RED ONION   SCALLION   GARLIC

ONIONS AND GARLIC *(left) are basics, although the garlic could be omitted. Red onions are used for extra color density and flavor.*
BLACK OLIVES *(below) add all the unique flavor of olive oil for a fraction of the calories.*

PAPRIKA   TURMERIC

CUMIN   CORIANDER

CHILIES, *fresh or dried, add zest. The hotter the chilies, the hotter the infusion. Seeding and ribbing reduces their heat.*
SUN-DRIED TOMATOES *add a caramelized smokiness. Choose dry-packed varieties.*

RED CHILIES   GREEN CHILIES   RED PEPPER FLAKES   SUN-DRIED TOMATOES   BLACK OLIVES

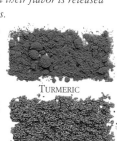

CARROT   FENNEL   PEPPERS   CELERY

VEGETABLES *contribute taste, texture, and valuable nutrition. Among the most frequently used in flavor infusions are carrots, fennel, peppers (red, yellow, or orange for a sweeter flavor), and celery.*

STOCK   RED WINE   BALSAMIC VINEGAR   TERIYAKI SAUCE   WORCESTERSHIRE SAUCE

BASIC LIQUIDS *of flavor infusions are good quality stocks (chicken, vegetable, or fish, depending on the recipe) and wines (red, white, vermouth, or sherry). Drizzles of aromatic and intense liquids such as vinegars and spicy sauces can be added for even deeper flavor.*

MAKING A FLAVOR INFUSION

For a basic flavor infusion, as in Tomato Sauce (see page 66), the ingredients are simmered, covered first to soften the onions, then uncovered to reduce the liquid.

TOMATO SAUCE INFUSION INGREDIENTS

2 red onions, chopped

4 sun-dried tomatoes, chopped

4 black olives, slivered off their pits

pinch or two of crushed red pepper flakes

4 garlic cloves

¼ cup (175ml) stock

¼ cup (175ml) red wine

1 Simmer these ingredients briskly until tender and the liquid has almost gone. This concentrates the flavor intensely.

2 Add the remaining Tomato Sauce ingredients (see page 66), except the herbs, in stages to the infusion and simmer to a thick sauce.

3 If the sauce is to be used at once, add the herbs. If the sauce is to be frozen, omit the herbs until it is to be used.

SIMMERING THE FLAVOR INFUSION ingredients uncovered (*above*) concentrates the flavor before the remaining Tomato Sauce ingredients are added (*left*). Plenty of fresh herbs give the finished sauce freshness and even more crisp flavor.

OTHER WAYS TO PREPARE FLAVOR INFUSIONS

STIR-FRYING: with this method, as in Cauliflower Stir-Fried in Red Wine (see page 69), the flavor infusion ingredients are initially stir-fried very quickly. They reach tenderness in the final stages.

BRAISING: as in Chicken Breasts with Braised Prunes & Shallots (see page 87), the flavor infusion ingredients are braised in the pan in which the main ingredients have already been browned.

SAUTEING: this method involves using the flavor infusion ingredients in a sauté, as in Cajun Prawns (see page 100). In this case, the infusion is still quite liquid when the prawns are added.

PEPPERS & GARLIC

PEPPERS AND GARLIC are both particularly useful in low-fat cooking, creating rich, round flavor without adding fat. Stunningly attractive red and yellow peppers (green ones lack sweetness) make food beautiful and delicious, and they add valuable nutrients as well. Broiled and peeled, or peeled raw and then simmered or sautéed, or infused and sieved, they are exquisitely sweet and digestible. Garlic, especially when roasted or braised, adds texture and depth to soups, stews, and sauces.

SAUTEING PEPPERS

1 To prepare red or yellow peppers for sautéing, first cut them in half and remove the stems, ribs, and seeds. Cut the halves into their natural sections.

2 Using a swivel-bladed vegetable peeler, which removes vegetable skins very thinly and thus saves valuable nutrients (*left*), peel the skin off the pepper sections. Without its skin, pepper flesh cooks to melting, sweet, and digestible tenderness.

3 For sautéing, dice the peeled pepper sections or cut into strips, as in Silky Stir-Fried Sweet Pepper Strips (*below*; see page 71 for recipe), and sauté in hot stock. Gentle stirring with a wooden spoon ensures that the pepper pieces do not break up as they cook.

A well-flavored stock replaces fat or oil as the medium for low-fat sautéing.

INFUSING PEPPERS

1 For sauces, e.g., Pepper Sauce (see page 64), simmer unpeeled pepper pieces in an infusion until soft. Pour into a blender.

2 Puree the peppers and the greatly reduced infusion in the blender into a thick sauce.

3 To remove the indigestible pepper skins, push the sauce through a sieve.

BROILING PEPPERS

1 Cut peppers in half, seed them, and flatten the pieces slightly. Broil under a hot broiler until charred and blackened.

2 Put the hot pepper halves in a covered bowl or plastic bag for a few minutes. This makes the skins easier to remove.

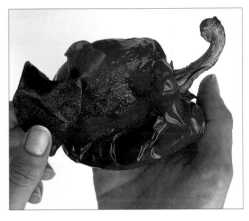

3 Strip off the blackened skins. Use the wonderfully smoky-flavored peppers as they are or as a cooking ingredient.

PREPARING GARLIC

CRUSH GARLIC with a wooden mallet. Hit separated cloves lightly to loosen the skins. Remove skins, then beat cloves to a pulp.

TO ROAST GARLIC, take a whole, firm, non-sprouting head of garlic and remove its papery outer covering. Do not separate the cloves. Slice off the pointed end. Wrap the whole head of garlic in foil, shiny side in, and roast in an oven preheated to 375°F/190°C, until the garlic turns into a puree (about 45 minutes). Cool the head of garlic (*left*), then separate the cloves and squeeze out the puree. Use the puree in recipes calling for garlic or simply – and unforgettably – as a spread for fresh, crusty bread.

EGGPLANT

WITHOUT THIS GLORIOUS, GLOSSY PURPLE VEGETABLE, low-fat cooking would be much less interesting. Eggplant makes the leanest of ground meat – usually dry, juiceless, and unrewarding when cooked – juicy and succulent, and it stretches meat so that a small amount goes a long way. It does these things directly, deliciously, with no conflicting flavor or off-putting texture. The overall impression of a meat dish with eggplant added will be that it is lighter, but not at all insubstantial.

USING RAW EGGPLANT

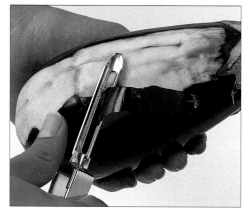

1 Use a swivel-bladed vegetable peeler to remove the skin from the eggplant as thinly as possible.

2 Trim the peeled eggplant and use a long-bladed knife to cut it lengthwise into slices about ½in (1cm) thick.

3 Cut the slices across into evenly shaped cubes. The eggplant is now ready for use in flavor infusions.

4 Cubes of eggplant are the main ingredient in the flavor infusion for Bolognese Sauce (*left*, and see page 62). Cooked in an infusion, eggplant becomes meltingly tender, and the cubes soak up the flavors like little sponges.

Cubes of eggplant cook gently among the flavor infusion ingredients for Bolognese Sauce.

ROASTING EGGPLANTS

1 Pierce the skin of a whole eggplant with a skewer. Bake on a baking sheet in an oven preheated to 350°F/180°C until it is browned, soft, and collapsed (about 40 minutes for an average-size eggplant).

2 Put the eggplant on a wire rack until it has cooled sufficiently for you to handle it. Strip off the skin with your fingers and discard it. Trim off the stem and top.

3 Cut the eggplant, first into slices lengthwise, then across into cubes. Because it is so soft, the eggplant quickly becomes a rough puree. If you prefer, puree it briefly in a food processor or blender. (Don't over-puree it.)

4 The roasted eggplant puree is now ready to be added, as a meat extender, to recipes like Spicy, Citrus-Scented Mexican Sausages (see page 94) or (*as above*) to Piquant Lemon Herb Meatballs (see page 95).

EQUIPMENT

MODERN, HEAVY-BOTTOMED, NONSTICK cookware makes low-fat cooking easier and more efficient than it used to be. The recipes in this book use a wide selection of nonstick pans along with a few well-chosen machines. A blender, for instance, is perfect for making vegetable puree sauces, and a food processor quickly makes pâtés, dips, and dessert toppings. Add to these a good assortment of the usual kitchen standbys, including whisks, bowls, measuring utensils, and top-quality tools, and cooking becomes a great pleasure.

JELLY-ROLL PAN, *or baking sheet (left), is nonstick and ideal for baking Chocolate Roulade (see page 118) or the sheet cake for Cassata (see page 143).*

LOAF PAN *(left), also nonstick, is ideal for baking tea breads.*

MUFFIN PAN *(left), for perfectly baked Spoonbread Corn Muffins (see page 154).*

TART PAN *with a removable base (left) is useful for baking clafouti, whether sweet or savory.*

CAKE PAN *(right), with a non-stick finish, is used to bake several recipes in this book.*

BAKING PARCHMENT *(below, left) requires no greasing before cookies or meringues are spooned or piped onto it.*

BAKING SHEET *with a nonstick coating (below) has a wide variety of uses, from roasting eggplant to baking cookies.*

ANGEL FOOD CAKE PAN *(above) is a must for baking Angel Cake (see page 143).*

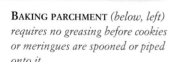

KITCHEN GADGETS

Well-chosen kitchen equipment, with such basics as sieves, wooden spoons, kitchen knives, measuring cups and spoons, scales, and a range of glass bowls and baking dishes, makes low-fat cooking efficient.

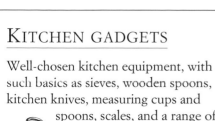

SIEVE

WOODEN SPOON

GLASS BOWL   PLASTIC SPRAY BOTTLE   BLENDER   FOOD PROCESSOR

BLENDER *is ideal for processing soups and sauces to exactly the right consistency.*

OIL-WATER SPRAY, *an essential of low-fat cooking, is easily and inexpensively made in a plastic spray bottle; look for clean, new, plant misters or scent spray bottles.*

FOOD PROCESSOR *mixes dry ingredients, chops vegetables and fruits, whips up purees, pâtés, and dips, and makes instant ice creams and sorbets.*

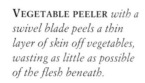

WOODEN MALLET *(or the wooden end of a steak tenderizing mallet) is ideal for loosening the skin of a garlic clove and then crushing it to a pulp.*

VEGETABLE PEELER *with a swivel blade peels a thin layer of skin off vegetables, wasting as little as possible of the flesh beneath.*

CAKE TESTER *tests cakes, of course, and doubles as a skewer for piercing vegetables such as eggplant and potatoes before baking.*

NONSTICK WOK AND STEAMER: *use the wok for no-fat stir-frying and sautéing, and the combination of wok and steamer for steaming and smoking. Choose a wok with a tight-fitting lid.*

SKILLET *with a nonstick surface allows foods to be sautéed in stock and wine rather than in fats or oils. A pan with a diameter of 12in (30cm) is a good, all-purpose size.*

OMELET PAN *with a nonstick surface allows omelets and other dishes to cook very quickly with no need to grease the pan.*

GRILL PAN *with nonstick ridges grills meat, poultry, and vegetables on top of the stove. It imparts a smoky, barbecue flavor and characteristic hatchmarks.*

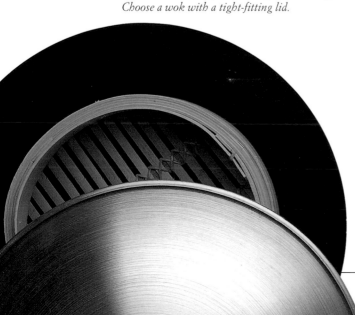

INGREDIENTS

THE EXCITEMENT OF THIS SPECIAL KIND of cooking lies in the lack of added fats and oils and high-fat dairy products, not only for the obvious health benefits but for the fresh vibrancy and depth of flavor that results from their absence. A surfeit of fatty, greasy ingredients is cloying; it clogs the tastebuds and muddles the balance of flavors. Without the glut of fat, the panoply of fresh and natural ingredients that forms the basis of this cuisine shines through in all its glory. Certain ingredients are used repeatedly. They are as important to the basic techniques of this cuisine as butter, oil, animal fats, and cream are to traditional cuisines.

VEGETABLES

Vegetables are vital to the techniques of this low-fat cuisine. They add color, nutrition, texture, bulk, and flavor. Nutritionally and sensually, they are a primary reason why this discipline works so well and the food is so satisfying.

GARLIC, *mellow and melting, roasted or pan-braised, adds texture and complexity. It is also used crushed and stock-sautéed.*

CHILIES *come in all sizes and degrees of heat. Often, smaller means hotter. Remove seeds and ribs for less heat. Red pepper flakes are useful.*

CANNED BEANS *come in many varieties (above are lima beans), and cut out the soaking and simmering dried beans need.*

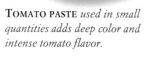

PASSATA *is sieved tomato; not as thick or intense as tomato paste.*

BLACK OLIVES *in brine, bottled or vacuum-packed, are slivered off their pits and used in infusions for a fraction of the fat of olive oil.*

EGGPLANT *is a magic ingredient. Roast, peel, and puree, then use to stretch extra-lean ground meat and make it succulent, or chop and use in an infusion. It will resonate with flavor.*

TOMATO PASTE *used in small quantities adds deep color and intense tomato flavor.*

DRIED MUSHROOMS *(porcini) soaked in warm water make a powerful wild mushroom stock for flavor infusions. Strain to remove grit.*

CANNED PEPPERS *in brine, drained, are a quick and good-looking replacement for freshly broiled peeled peppers.*

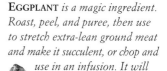

PEPPERS *are endlessly useful, either raw and peeled for sautés and infusions, or broiled and peeled for smoky purees and sauces.*

CANNED TOMATOES, *whole or chopped, are used in sauces, soups, casseroles, and stews.*

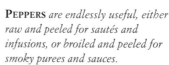

SUN-DRIED TOMATOES, *dry-packed, snipped into an infusion, give a deep, smoky, caramelized taste.*

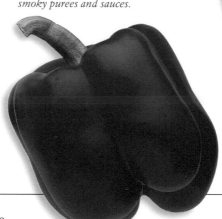

SAUCES

Several bottled sauces are invaluable shortcuts to building complex flavor. They can be used as seasoning, in infusions, or in marinades. Always use in small amounts so that they do not overpower other ingredients in the recipe.

HOISIN SAUCE *is often referred to as "Chinese barbecue sauce."*

WORCESTERSHIRE SAUCE *is unique and anchovy-spiked. It pairs well with Tabasco.*

TABASCO SAUCE, *made with peppers, is piquant and zippy, for fans of edible fire.*

TERIYAKI SAUCE *adds depth. If you cannot find it, use soy sauce.*

OILS & VINEGARS

Oils, in tiny amounts in the oil-water spray, are used for seasoning, for lubrication, and to prevent sticking. Vinegars add a tang to low-fat dishes.

OLIVE OIL *has incomparable flavor. Use the best extra-virgin olive oil.*

SUNFLOWER OIL *is used when a neutral flavor is needed.*

SESAME OIL *flavors Asian dishes. As always, only a spritz is needed.*

SAFFLOWER OIL, *like sunflower oil, is used for a neutral taste.*

BALSAMIC VINEGAR *is rich and sweet-and-sour.*

OLIVE OIL   SUNFLOWER OIL   SESAME OIL   SAFFLOWER OIL   BALSAMIC VINEGAR

HERBS

Nothing compares with the pungent intensity of fresh herbs. Mix and match to taste.

BASIL *has a spicy flavor, with hints of clove and pepper. It is delicious with garlic, lemon, and tomatoes.*

FLAT-LEAF PARSLEY *has more flavor than the curly variety.*

ROSEMARY *has pungent needles, to be cooked rather than used as a garnish.*

CILANTRO *has an unusual, almost musty taste. Once you get used to it, you'll adore it.*

MINT *is splendid in savory recipes as well as sweet, and epitomizes freshness.*

SPICES

Mixtures of ground spices, simmered in an infusion with other ingredients, give a well-rounded flavor.

DIJON MUSTARDS *and flavored mustards add an interesting dimension to recipes and stabilize low-fat yogurt.*

TURMERIC *has lovely color and a bracing freshness.*

PAPRIKA *varies in taste from mildly hot to mild and sweet.*

CHILI POWDER *(cayenne) is pure ground chilies and should be used with care.*

CORIANDER SEEDS, *ground, have a different taste from the fresh leaves.*

FRESH GINGER ROOT *should be sliced, peeled, and crushed with a wooden mallet.*

DAIRY PRODUCTS

There are superb medium-fat and skim milk dairy products available, providing rich creaminess without the heavy cloying effect of full-fat products. Use in sauces, dips, and – most exciting – desserts. Since many of the products they replace are 80 percent fat, the dairy products here are to be cherished.

QUARK *is smooth, creamy, and skimmed (0% fat), slightly tangy but not sour, and wonderful in all sorts of recipes.*

RICOTTA *is sweet and creamy, 14% fat, and a perfect substitute for much higher fat crème fraîche, whipped cream, and mascarpone.*

MOZZARELLA *(low-fat version is 10% fat) melts beautifully. It is mild and milky.*

SKIM MILK POWDER *is fortified with fat-soluble vitamins A and D. Add it to skim milk for extra body, richness, and nutrition.*

SKIM MILK *seems richer when it is mixed with skim milk powder. Use it in soups and sauces and for luscious puddings.*

LOW-FAT YOGURT *can be drained in a cheesecloth-lined sieve; it will be as thick as the higher fat kind.*

FROMAGE FRAIS *is made from cultured skim milk. Thick, creamy, and slightly tangy, it replaces sour cream, crème fraîche, and cream.*

WINES

Red and white wines and fortified wines combine with stock to form the basic sauté liquid that replaces butter and oils. In simmering, the alcohol evaporates, but full-bodied flavor remains. Small amounts of various liqueurs give fragrance to desserts.

RED WINE *should be a decent, drinkable dry red, not too expensive.*

WHITE WINE *to choose is a dry white for a lighter effect.*

AMARETTO *has a delicate almond fragrance, excellent in desserts.*

SHERRY *is perfect in mushroom sautés and sauces and bean soups.*

COINTREAU *mixed with orange juice and vanilla is exquisite in desserts.*

VERMOUTH, *with its herby bouquet, is a fabulous cooking ingredient.*

RED WINE

WHITE WINE

AMARETTO

SHERRY

VERMOUTH

COINTREAU

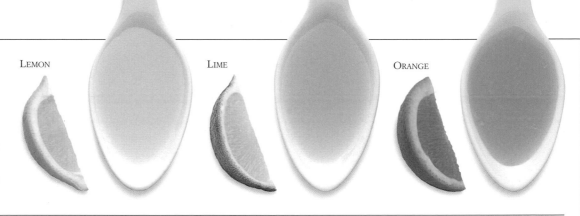

JUICES

Citrus juices are important for their tenderizing properties and the spark that their acid edge brings. Grated citrus zest (the skin without the underlying bitter white pith) is important as well.

LEMON

LIME

ORANGE

DESSERTS

Rich-tasting low-fat desserts are possible when you use the full range of low-fat dairy products, and add other well-chosen goodies: low-fat cocoa powder, the best high-cocoa-solid chocolate, fragrant liqueurs, perfectly ripe fruit, preserves. I like old-fashioned desserts brought up-to-date with a fresher, lighter profile. Bread puddings, rice puddings, crumbles, clafoutis, even tiramisù will take on a new, more modern character.

SEMISWEET CHOCOLATE *to choose is one with at least 70% cocoa solids.*

COCOA POWDER *should be low-fat; it is intensely chocolaty.*

CORNSTARCH *is sometimes used in small amounts to thicken sauces.*

GRAPE NUTS® *cereal crushed with amaretti makes a splendid crumb crust.*

AMARETTI *to choose are those flavored with apricot kernels, rather than high-fat almonds.*

DRIED PEARS *make a delicious addition to dried fruit compotes.*

DRIED PEACHES *can be used in compotes, puddings, and in baking.*

VANILLA EXTRACT

DRIED APRICOTS *are almost more palatable than the fresh fruit and are good in desserts and baking.*

DRIED FIGS *are another excellent dried fruit. Eat them as they are or use in desserts and baking.*

DRIED CHERRIES, *along with raisins, dried blueberries, and cranberries, are dessert basics.*

VANILLA *in bean and extract (not the harsh essence) form is much used. Scrape the seeds from the bean and use as flavoring; reuse the bean.*

VANILLA BEAN

PRESERVES *are often used in place of sugar for a more interesting balance of flavor.*

MARMALADE *is another delicious sweetener that can be used instead of sugar.*

HONEY *can be whisked into fromage frais for a gorgeous, creamy topping.*

PHYLLO PASTRY *has delicate layers that can be coated with purchased oil spray instead of the traditional butter.*

APRICOT

BLUEBERRY

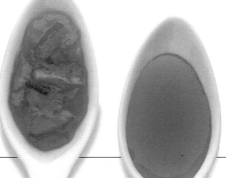

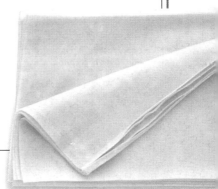

RECIPES

HERE IS LOW-FAT COOKING TO CHERISH: MORE
THAN 150 RECIPES IN WHICH A WIDE-RANGING CHOICE OF
THE WORLD'S FINEST INGREDIENTS ARE LAVISHED ON AN
EXHILARATING ARRAY OF DISHES DESIGNED TO DELIGHT THE
TASTE BUDS AND SATISFY EVERY APPETITE. RECIPES FOR
SALADS, SNACKS, AND APPETIZERS PROVIDE OPPORTUNITIES
FOR GUILT-FREE SNACKING BETWEEN MEALS. THERE
IS A SPLENDID RANGE OF MAIN COURSE DISHES, USING MEAT,
POULTRY, FISH, VEGETABLES, PASTA, AND GRAINS, AND A
MOUTHWATERING COLLECTION OF DESSERTS AND BAKED
GOODS, INCLUDING BREADS, CAKES, AND COOKIES.

SOUPS & APPETIZERS

AN ARRAY OF CROSTINI, served with a selection of dips and spreads, is an inspiring way to begin a meal for those who love lots of color and texture. Soup is also a marvelous way to get things going. With a variety of vegetables, spices, herbs, and flavor infusions, building complex layers of flavor into soup is one of the most satisfying of kitchen activities. I put it right up there with breadmaking. In fact, crostini and soup are such perfect companions, and such a feast of good nutrition, that the meal need go no further.

—— FRAGRANT VEGETABLE SOUP ——

Another name for this recipe could be "New Wave minestrone" – it is as good a way as any to describe this gently spiced, lime-spiked combination of vegetables, herbs, and tiny pasta shapes.

INGREDIENTS

1 red onion, roughly chopped

1 carrot, halved lengthwise, then cut across into chunks

1 yellow and 1 red pepper, peeled, seeded, and chopped (see page 34)

1 red chili, seeded and finely chopped

juice of 1 lime

grated zest of ¼ lime

1 tsp ground cumin

½ tsp ground paprika

7½ cups (1.8 liters) vegetable stock (see page 30)

1lb (500g) potatoes, peeled and cut into 1in (2.5cm) chunks

1 fennel bulb, 1lb (500g), halved and cut into 1in (2.5cm) chunks

14oz (425g) canned tomatoes, well drained and cut into strips

8oz (250g) frozen corn kernels

2 zucchini, about 6oz (180g) each, halved lengthwise and cut across into 1in (2.5cm) slices

1 tbsp tomato paste

juice of ½ large orange

½ cup (60g) tiny soup pasta

several dashes of Tabasco sauce, to taste (optional)

salt and freshly ground black pepper

chopped flat-leaf parsley, to garnish

1 Put the onion, carrot, peppers, chili, half the lime juice and all the zest, spices, and 1¼ cups (300ml) stock in a heavy-bottomed saucepan. Cover, bring to a boil, and simmer briskly for 10 minutes.

2 Uncover the pan and add another ⅔ cup (150ml) of the stock, the potatoes, and the fennel. Simmer briskly for 6–8 minutes, until the liquid is almost gone and the vegetables are half-cooked. Stir in the tomatoes and season. Stir in ½ cup (125ml) of the stock, simmer for 4–5 minutes, then stir in the corn and zucchini. Simmer for 3–4 minutes.

3 Put 3 tablespoons of the soup mixture (excluding potato or zucchini pieces) in a blender with the tomato paste and 3–4 tablespoons stock and blend to a smooth puree. Stir back into the soup and bring to a simmer. Add the remaining stock, lime juice, and orange juice. Add the soup pasta and Tabasco sauce, if using.

4 Simmer for 7–10 minutes, partially covered, until the pasta is tender. Taste, adding salt and pepper and a few drops of citrus juice, or Tabasco, as needed. Stir in the parsley. Serve the soup topped with a spoonful of Grilled Pepper & Oregano Pistou (see page 65), if desired.

Per serving

Total fat (g)	3
Saturated fat (g)	1
Unsaturated fat (g)	2
Cholesterol (mg)	0
Sodium (mg)	327
Calories	260

Makes
6 servings

FRAGRANT VEGETABLE SOUP
*is a lightly spiced mix of many kinds
of colorful vegetables and tiny
soup pasta shapes.*

RED BEAN, GRILLED PEPPER & EGGPLANT SOUP

A color-contrasted swirl of yellow pepper puree makes a dramatic garnish to this bowl of velvety soup.

INGREDIENTS

2½ cups (600ml) Tomato Eggplant Sauce (page 62)

four 14oz (425g) cans red kidney beans, drained and rinsed

2½ cups (600ml) stock (see page 30)

several dashes of Tabasco sauce

several dashes of Worcestershire sauce

salt and freshly ground black pepper

1 red pepper, broiled (see page 35)

1 yellow pepper, broiled (see page 35)

½ tsp Sambal Oelek (hot chili condiment)

1 Put the sauce, beans, and stock in a saucepan and season with the Tabasco and Worcestershire sauces, plus salt and pepper to taste. Simmer for 10 minutes. Let cool slightly.

2 Cut the red pepper into pieces and add (with any juices) to the soup. Puree the soup in the blender in batches until it is a velvety smooth texture.

3 Puree the yellow pepper with the Sambal Oelek. Serve the soup in soup plates with a swirl of the yellow pepper puree on top.

 Per serving

Total fat (g)	2
Saturated fat (g)	1
Unsaturated fat (g)	1
Cholesterol (mg)	0
Sodium (mg)	1077
Calories	295

 Makes
6 servings

SPICY SWEET POTATO BISQUE

Breathtaking color, compelling texture, and lots of pizzazz make this a soup to relish. Its creamy texture is amazing when you consider that it contains no cream, indeed, no dairy products at all. It is a testimony to the versatility of vegetable purees.

INGREDIENTS

6¼ cups (1.5 liters) vegetable stock (see page 30)

juice of 2 limes

2 red onions, chopped

6 large garlic cloves, crushed

one ½in (1cm) piece fresh ginger, peeled and crushed

4 sun-dried tomatoes, chopped

1–2 pinches crushed red pepper flakes

½ tsp ground turmeric

1 tsp ground cumin

½ tsp ground coriander

1lb (500g) baking potatoes, peeled and cut into chunks

2lb (1kg) orange-fleshed sweet potatoes, peeled and cut into chunks

several dashes of Tabasco sauce

salt and freshly ground black pepper

chopped fresh chives, to garnish

1 Put 1¼ cups (300ml) of the stock, the juice of 1 lime, the onions, garlic, ginger, sun-dried tomatoes, crushed red pepper flakes, and spices in a heavy-bottomed saucepan. Cover and bring to a brisk simmer. Uncover and simmer until the liquid is almost gone and the onions are cooking in their own juices.

2 Add all the potatoes and stir over moderate heat until they begin to catch a little, and are well coated with the onions, garlic, and spices. Stir in the remaining stock and several dashes of Tabasco sauce. Simmer, partially covered, for 15 minutes or so, until the potatoes are very tender.

3 If you have an immersion blender, put it into the pot and puree the soup. Otherwise, cool the soup slightly and puree in batches in an ordinary blender, holding down the cover. The soup should be smooth and velvety. Return the puree to the pan and add the remaining lime juice and more stock, if it seems too thick. Taste and add salt, pepper, and more Tabasco, as needed. Serve garnished with chopped chives.

 Per serving

Total fat (g)	1
Saturated fat (g)	<1
Unsaturated fat (g)	<1
Cholesterol (mg)	0
Sodium (mg)	306
Calories	277

 Makes
6 servings

White Bean, Sweet Potato & Fennel Soup

More a vegetable stew than a soup, this spicy bowlful of goodness would make a great meal with garlic bread. To make a creamy soup, puree the slightly cooled soup in a blender. Return to the pan, add stock to thin it a little, and season.

INGREDIENTS

3¾ cups (900ml) stock (see page 30)

½ cup (125ml) Amontillado sherry

2 fennel bulbs, trimmed and chopped

6 scallions, trimmed and sliced

1 zucchini, about ¼lb (125g), trimmed and roughly chopped

1 orange-fleshed sweet potato, peeled and roughly chopped

2 garlic cloves, crushed

one ¼in (5mm) slice fresh ginger, peeled and crushed

1 red chili, seeded and chopped

1 tsp ground turmeric

1 tsp ground paprika

1½ tsp ground cumin

1½ tsp ground coriander

juice of 1 orange

juice of ½ lime

two 13oz (400g) cans cannellini beans, rinsed and drained

1 yellow pepper, broiled, peeled (see page 35) and diced

salt and freshly ground black pepper

chopped fresh parsley and cilantro, to garnish

1 Put 1¼ cups (300ml) of the stock in a heavy-bottomed saucepan or wok. Add the sherry, fennel, scallions, zucchini, sweet potato, garlic, ginger, chili, spices, and citrus juices. Cover and boil for 5 minutes. Remove the cover and simmer briskly, until the vegetables are tender and cooking in their juices.

2 Stir in the beans and pepper, with any juices. Season with salt and pepper, pour in the remaining stock, and simmer for 5 minutes. Cool slightly.

3 Ladle 1¼ cups (300ml) of the soup into a blender and blend until smooth. Stir back into the soup. Bring to a simmer, taste, and adjust the seasonings, if necessary. Serve strewn with herbs.

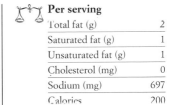

Per serving

Total fat (g)	2
Saturated fat (g)	1
Unsaturated fat (g)	1
Cholesterol (mg)	0
Sodium (mg)	697
Calories	200

Makes
6 servings

BUTTERNUT SQUASH, GINGER & LIME PUREE

This blazingly orange puree is smooth, rich, and spicy. Spread it on the best bread as part of a selection of crostini, or serve it as a dip or in little pots at the table, instead of butter.

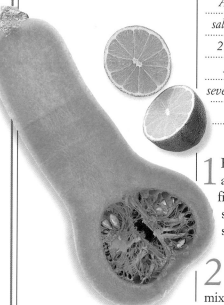

INGREDIENTS

1 butternut squash

oil-water spray (see page 29)

2 large garlic cloves

1in (2.5cm) piece fresh ginger, peeled

Amontillado sherry (see method)

salt and freshly ground black pepper

2 tbsp buttermilk or fromage frais

several dashes of Tabasco sauce

several dashes of Worcestershire sauce

juice of ½ lime

1 Halve the squash lengthwise and scrape out the seeds and fiber. Oil-water spray the cut side of each half and put, cut side up, on a baking sheet.

2 Crush together the garlic and ginger and put half the mixture into each squash half. Fill each cavity three-quarters full with sherry. Season each half with salt and plenty of pepper.

3 Roast the squash halves in a preheated oven for 45 minutes, or until the flesh is very tender. Several times during the baking, dip a pastry brush in the cavities and brush the tops of the squash with the sherry (when the squash is tender, the sherry will have almost evaporated).

4 Remove from the oven and let cool, draped with a clean dish towel.

5 Scrape the squash pulp and ginger-garlic mixture into a food processor. Add the remaining ingredients. Process until very smooth. Taste and add more salt, pepper, lime juice, Tabasco, or Worcestershire sauce, as needed.

 Per recipe quantity

Total fat (g)	2
Saturated fat (g)	<1
Unsaturated fat (g)	1
Cholesterol (mg)	1
Sodium (mg)	70
Calories	268

 Oven temperature
400°F/200°C

 Baking time
45 minutes

 Makes
2½ cups (600ml)

GREEN PEA GUACAMOLE

I've been substituting peas for avocado to make a fresh and herby low-fat version of guacamole ever since I read Michael Robert's brilliant suggestion in Secret Ingredients. *Use the best brand of bottled salsa you can find. Illustrated on page 61.*

INGREDIENTS

1–2 large garlic cloves, crushed

1 tbsp lime juice

1 tbsp lemon juice

1lb (500g) frozen petits pois, thawed

2 tbsp chopped parsley

2 tbsp chopped cilantro

1 tbsp shredded mint

1–2 tbsp Mexican salsa (choose medium or hot according to your taste)

salt

1 Put the garlic in a glass bowl or cup. Add the lime and lemon juices and allow to marinate for 10 minutes.

2 Put the garlic mixture, petits pois, herbs, and Mexican salsa into a food processor. Add salt to taste and process to an almost smooth texture. Taste again and add more lime juice, Mexican salsa, and salt, as needed.

VARIATION

For a simple pea puree, simmer together 1lb (500g) thawed petits pois, 1½ cups (350ml) stock, 2 lightly crushed garlic cloves, and the juice of ½ lime until the peas are cooked but still bright green. Puree in a blender until velvety smooth. Season with salt and pepper and stir in a tablespoon of torn, fresh mint. Add the juice of the leftover half lime, if desired.

 Per recipe quantity

Total fat (g)	5
Saturated fat (g)	1
Unsaturated fat (g)	4
Cholesterol (mg)	0
Sodium (mg)	175
Calories	267

 Makes
2½ cups (600ml)

HOISIN-LEMON RUBY BEET SPREAD

Oven-roasted beets, roughly pureed and laced with flavorings that augment and counterpoint their earthiness, make a glowing spread.

INGREDIENTS

½lb (250g) oven-roasted beets, cut into chunks (see page 78)

1½ tbsp hoisin sauce

2 tbsp lemon juice

Put all the ingredients in a food processor and process to a slightly rough puree. Taste, and add a little more hoisin sauce and lemon juice, if needed.

VARIATION

Replace the hoisin sauce with a purchased hot mango chutney, added to taste.

 Per recipe quantity

Total fat (g)	1
Saturated fat (g)	neg
Unsaturated fat (g)	1
Cholesterol (mg)	0
Sodium (mg)	462
Calories	133

Makes
1¼ cups (300ml)

SWEET POTATO SPREAD

Another smooth, rich, and vivid puree to spread on bread or use as a dip. The sweet potato takes on a buttery, creamy texture, and the spices and citrus juices set off its sweetness perfectly.

INGREDIENTS

1 sweet potato, about ¾lb (425g)

2 large garlic cloves, crushed

3 sun-dried tomatoes, chopped

½–1 chili, seeded and chopped

½ tbsp turmeric

½ tsp ground cumin

½ tsp ground coriander

½ tsp paprika

juice of ½ lime

2 tbsp lemon juice

1¼ cups (300ml) stock (see page 30)

1–2 tbsp buttermilk or fromage frais

salt and freshly ground black pepper

1 Pierce the potato in several places with a thin skewer. Bake in a preheated oven, directly on the oven shelf, until tender.

2 Meanwhile, put the remaining ingredients except the buttermilk and salt and pepper in a skillet, and simmer briskly until the liquid is almost gone.

3 Split the sweet potato and scrape the flesh into a food processor. Add the spice mixture, buttermilk, and seasoning. Process to a smooth, buttery puree. Taste and adjust the seasonings and citrus juices, as needed.

 Per recipe quantity

Total fat (g)	4
Saturated fat (g)	1
Unsaturated fat (g)	3
Cholesterol (mg)	<1
Sodium (mg)	473
Calories	467

 Oven temperature:
400°F/200°C

Baking time
about 45 minutes

Makes
1 cup (250ml)

WILD MUSHROOM PATE

This is a deep, dark pâté. It is splendid spread on the best crusty bread you can find, either as part of a selection of crostini or on its own.

INGREDIENTS

1 quantity Mushrooms Made Wild (see page 74)

1 tsp spicy Dijon mustard

few drops of lemon juice

Put all the ingredients in the bowl of a food processor and process to a dark, rough puree, adding more lemon juice to taste.

 Per serving

Total fat (g)	1
Saturated fat (g)	neg
Unsaturated fat (g)	1
Cholesterol (mg)	0
Sodium (mg)	123
Calories	53

Makes
4 servings

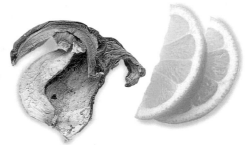

TUNA & CHUTNEY DIP

This is an interestingly spicy dip or spread that makes the most of a can of tuna. Canned tuna is one of the sublime pantry ingredients, as are good jarred chutneys. Always buy the best quality you can find of both.

INGREDIENTS

one 12oz (375g) can dark tuna in brine, well drained

1 heaping tbsp hot mango chutney

1 heaping tbsp tomato chutney

1 tbsp very low-fat fromage frais

Put all the ingredients in a food processor and process to a smooth puree. Let the mixture stand for at least an hour for the flavors to develop. To serve, spread on crusty bread, or use as a dip with vegetable crudités. This is particularly good with steamed, cooled, new potatoes.

Per recipe quantity

Total fat (g)	2
Saturated fat (g)	1
Unsaturated fat (g)	1
Cholesterol (mg)	179
Sodium (mg)	1381
Calories	403

Makes
1¼ cups (300ml)

HERBED RAITA

INGREDIENTS

handful of chopped fresh dill, thyme, and tarragon

2 cups (475g) very low-fat yogurt or fromage frais

zest of ½ lemon, grated

Stir the three herbs into the yogurt or fromage frais, then add the lemon zest and stir until thoroughly combined.

VARIATIONS

Use whichever herbs sound good to you: chives and parsley; mint and coriander; basil and flat-leaf parsley; or mint with peeled, seeded, grated cucumber. To make things even more interesting, add crushed garlic marinated in a little wine vinegar. For a thicker raita, first drain the yogurt or fromage frais through a cheesecloth-lined sieve (see page 124).

Per recipe quantity

Total fat (g)	<1
Saturated fat (g)	<1
Unsaturated fat (g)	neg
Cholesterol (mg)	10
Sodium (mg)	401
Calories	192

Makes
2 cups (600ml)

CREAMY CORN DIP

Santa Fe pesto is how I think of this lively, creamy dip. Corn, roasted garlic, chilies, and herbs imbue the Quark/ricotta mixture with ineffable new-world flavor.

INGREDIENTS

12oz (375g) can corn kernels, drained

½–1 chili, seeded and finely chopped

8oz (250g) Quark (if unavailable, use all ricotta, 17oz (525g) in total recipe)

9oz (275g) ricotta

4 tbsp grated Parmesan

pulp from 1 head of roasted (or braised) garlic (see page 35)

salt and freshly ground black pepper

3 tbsp chopped fresh parsley

3 tbsp snipped fresh chives

1 Put the corn and chili in a food processor and process to a very rough puree.

2 Add the Quark, ricotta, Parmesan, and garlic and season with salt and pepper. Process again until blended but not quite smooth.

3 Stir in the herbs and pulse a few times to combine. Cover with plastic wrap and chill until needed. Serve as a dip, a spread, or a garnish for thick soups – just drop a small mound on the surface of the soup.

Per recipe quantity

Total fat (g)	55
Saturated fat (g)	32
Unsaturated fat (g)	20
Cholesterol (mg)	200
Sodium (mg)	1997
Calories	1304

Makes
2½ cups (600ml)

POTATO SKIN DIPPERS

*C*risp potato skin wedges are superb with dips or all by themselves, or with just a shower of black pepper and a good squeeze of fresh lemon juice.

INGREDIENTS

2 large baking potatoes

oil-water spray (see page 29)

1 Scrub the potatoes and pat them dry, then cut them in half lengthwise.

2 Scoop out the insides, leaving a shell about ¼in (5mm) thick. (Save the scooped-out potato for another use, such as mashed potatoes or potato soup.) Cut each shell half lengthwise in half.

3 Oil-spray a nonstick baking sheet, put the potato quarters, skin side down, on the sheet, and spray lightly with oil-water spray. Bake in an oven preheated to 400°F/200°C for 25–35 minutes, until golden brown and very crisp. Serve at once.

 Per serving

Total fat (g)	<1
Saturated fat (g)	neg
Unsaturated fat (g)	neg
Cholesterol (mg)	0
Sodium (mg)	10
Calories	115

 Makes
2 servings

PITA CRISPS

*D*ips need dippers, and these pita triangles make particularly fine ones. They are quick and easy to make, and are virtually fat-free – so much better than high-fat fried dippers.

INGREDIENTS

1 pita bread (brown or white)

1 Cut the pita bread into quarters or eighths. Separate each piece into two.

2 Put the pieces, in a single layer, on a nonstick baking sheet. Bake in an oven preheated to 300°F/150°C for 10–15 minutes, or until the pieces of pita bread are dried out and crisp – fat-free crisp, in fact.

 Per serving

Total fat (g)	<1
Saturated fat (g)	neg
Unsaturated fat (g)	<1
Cholesterol (mg)	0
Sodium (mg)	156
Calories	80

 Makes
4 servings

SALADS & DRESSINGS

A LOW-FAT LIFESTYLE means no vinaigrette and no mayonnaise, the two high-fat staples of salad-making. But there is no need to make do with just an acetic squeeze of lemon juice. My nonfat vinaigrettes (a contradiction in terms, I know – no oil equals no vinaigrette, but I'm bending the rules here) dress salads with great style. Mixtures of exquisite vinegars and citrus juices can make lovely dressings, and my Not Mayo, based on fromage frais, stands in very successfully for the wickedly high-fat real thing.

ASPARAGUS WITH CREAMY SHRIMP DRESSING
mixes luxury ingredients for a superb salad.

DRESSING BASE

The rich, creamy dressing for this salad has an infusion of high-flavored ingredients as its base. Rapid simmering reduces the infusion to a thick pulp, which is mixed with lightly spiced fromage frais and shrimp.

LEMON JUICE

LEMON RIND

GARLIC

SCALLION

VEGETABLE STOCK

DRY VERMOUTH

TERIYAKI SAUCE

WORCESTERSHIRE SAUCE

ASPARAGUS WITH A CREAMY SHRIMP DRESSING

INGREDIENTS

2in (5cm) strip of lemon rind

1½ cups (350ml) stock (see page 30)

½ cup (125ml) dry vermouth

10 garlic cloves, lightly crushed

6 scallions, trimmed and chopped

lemon juice, to taste

dash or two each of teriyaki and Worcestershire sauces

1lb (500g) jumbo shrimp, peeled

2 tbsp fromage frais

1 tsp spicy Dijon mustard

dash of Tabasco sauce

salt and freshly ground black pepper

2–3 tbsp each chopped fresh basil and parsley

about 1lb (500g) asparagus, trimmed, peeled, and steamed (see page 78)

½ cucumber, peeled, seeded, and sliced into thin crescents

¾lb (300g) cherry tomatoes, halved

1 Put the lemon rind, 1¼ cups (300ml) of stock, the vermouth, garlic, scallions, a few drops of lemon juice, and the teriyaki and Worcestershire sauces in a pan. Bring to a boil, stirring occasionally, and cook until the garlic is tender and falling apart and the liquid is reduced to a glaze.

2 Discard the lemon rind. Take the pan off the heat and mash the mixture with a potato masher. Transfer to a bowl.

3 In the same pan (no need to wash it) bring the remaining stock with a few drops of lemon juice added to a boil. Add the shrimp and cook, stirring, for 2–3 minutes, until just done. Drain, refresh under cold water, and drain again.

4 Whisk the fromage frais with the mustard. Add a dash each of Tabasco and Worcestershire sauces, the garlic mixture, the shrimp, and seasonings. Fold in the herbs. Arrange the asparagus on a platter. Pile the creamy shrimp over the stem ends and arrange the cucumber and tomatoes all around.

Per main course serving	
Total fat (g)	2
Saturated fat (g)	<1
Unsaturated fat (g)	1
Cholesterol (mg)	244
Sodium (mg)	405
Calories	153

Makes
6 servings as a first course, 4 as a main course

ROASTED BEETS, ORANGE & ARUGULA SALAD

The earthy sweetness of the beets and the bitterness of the arugula in this salad, not to mention the dark red and the deep green, make a stunning combination.

INGREDIENTS

¼lb (125g) arugula leaves

four ¼lb (125g) oven-roasted beets (see page 78), peeled and sliced

2 blood oranges (or 2 ordinary seedless oranges), peeled and cut into thin slices

5 tbsp Beet Vinaigrette (see page 59)

salt and freshly ground black pepper

chopped fresh flat-leaf parsley, to garnish

1 Line a platter with arugula leaves. Slice the beets and overlap, interspersing with orange slices here and there, on the leaves.

2 Drizzle on the vinaigrette and season with salt and pepper. Garnish the salad with parsley before serving.

Per serving

Total fat (g)	<1
Saturated fat (g)	0
Unsaturated fat (g)	<1
Cholesterol (mg)	0
Sodium (mg)	129
Calories	85

Makes
4 servings

CANNELLINI BEAN & CHICKPEA SALAD

Another vibrantly colored salad, this is also quick to make since it combines two beans that are available in cans – no need to soak overnight.

INGREDIENTS

2 garlic cloves, crushed

½–1 chili pepper, seeded and finely diced

½ red onion, chopped

juice of 1 large orange

juice of 1 lime

2 tbsp lemon juice

pinch of sugar

1 tbsp balsamic vinegar

3 small carrots

1 large yellow pepper

2–3 inner celery stalks, leaves and all

4 small, ripe tomatoes

15oz (475g) can chickpeas, drained and rinsed

15oz (475g) can cannellini beans, drained and rinsed

salt and freshly ground black pepper

2oz (60g) baby spinach leaves

2oz (60g) watercress leaves

chopped fresh flat-leaf parsley and shredded mint, to garnish

1 Put the garlic, chili pepper, onion, citrus juices, sugar, and balsamic vinegar in a large bowl and stir together well. Let the dressing marinate while you prepare the vegetables.

2 Peel and dice the carrots, and skin, seed, and dice the pepper (see page 35). Peel and chop the celery, and seed and dice the tomatoes.

3 Toss the vegetables in the dressing in the bowl. Add the chickpeas and cannellini beans and stir with two spoons to mix well. Season with salt and pepper. Leave in the refrigerator for a few hours or overnight to allow the flavors to blend.

4 To serve, line a platter with baby spinach and watercress leaves. Heap the vegetables and beans on the leaves, and garnish with the herbs.

Per serving

Total fat (g)	3
Saturated fat (g)	<1
Unsaturated fat (g)	2
Cholesterol (mg)	0
Sodium (mg)	542
Calories	198

Makes
6 servings

COUSCOUS VEGETABLE SALAD

Couscous, mixed with one of the wonderful no-fat vinaigrettes and lavishly strewn with crisp vegetables, then surrounded by red onions and chilies, makes a visually dazzling side dish or vegetarian main course.

INGREDIENTS

For the couscous

1 cup (180g) couscous

1 cup (250ml) well-seasoned stock (see page 30)

For the relish

1 small red onion, finely chopped

1 chili, seeded and finely chopped

1 tbsp balsamic vinegar

juice of 1 lime and ½ orange

8–10 ripe tomatoes, cut into quarters or eighths

For the vegetables

½ cucumber, peeled, halved, seeded, and sliced

2 inner celery stalks with leaves, sliced

1 red pepper, skinned, seeded, and diced (see page 34)

1 yellow pepper, skinned, seeded, and diced (see page 34)

2 small zucchini, trimmed and diced

For the dressing and garnish

1 quantity Sun-Dried Tomato Vinaigrette (see Basic Vinaigrette variations, page 59)

1 tbsp each chopped fresh flat-leaf parsley and mint, to garnish

1 To make the couscous, bring the stock to a boil. Put the couscous in a bowl, then pour the stock over and mix well. Cover and leave for 10–15 minutes, until the couscous is tender and the liquid has been absorbed. Fluff with a fork.

2 Mix together all the relish ingredients except the tomatoes. Let marinate for 10 minutes.

3 For the vegetables, put all the prepared ingredients in a bowl, drizzle with 2–3 tablespoons of the dressing, and stir together gently with two spoons.

4 To assemble the salad, mix the couscous with half the vegetables and ⅔ cup (150ml) of the dressing. Pile onto a platter and surround with the remaining vegetables.

5 Gently mix together the relish mixture and the tomatoes and arrange on the outer perimeter of the platter, then sprinkle the freshly chopped parsley and mint over all.

 Per serving

Total fat (g)	2
Saturated fat (g)	neg
Unsaturated fat (g)	1
Cholesterol (mg)	0
Sodium (mg)	248
Calories	202

 Makes
4 servings

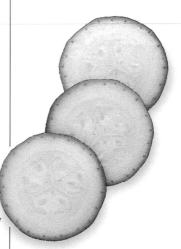

TOMATO, PEACH & BROILED PEPPER SALAD

I give specific quantities for the ingredients in this wonderfully colorful salad, but amounts can be varied to suit your own taste or what is in season.

INGREDIENTS

2 ripe tomatoes, sliced

2 ripe peaches, halved, pitted, and sliced

1 each red and orange peppers, broiled and skinned (see page 35)

salt and freshly ground black pepper

1 tbsp chopped fresh flat-leaf parsley

1 tbsp shredded fresh basil

½ quantity Broiled Pepper Vinaigrette (see page 59)

1 Alternate slices of tomato, peach, and broiled pepper on an attractive platter.

2 Season the salad lightly with salt and pepper, then sprinkle on the parsley and basil. Pass the vinaigrette separately.

 Per serving

Total fat (g)	1
Saturated fat (g)	neg
Unsaturated fat (g)	1
Cholesterol (mg)	0
Sodium (mg)	203
Calories	68

 Makes
4 servings

NOT MAYO

Real mayonnaise is an emulsion of egg yolk and oil – just thinking about it strikes terror in my heart. Instead, try this fromage frais dressing. Not mayo – no, indeed – but wonderfully useful, creamy, and delicious all the same, especially as a sandwich spread.

INGREDIENTS

1 tbsp Dijon mustard

1lb (500g) very low-fat fromage frais

Gently whisk the mustard into the fromage frais.

VARIATIONS

Flavored mustards work wonderfully too – try Red Pepper and Garlic Provençal Mustard instead of the basic Dijon mustard. The following may also be added (in small quantities at a time until you reach the flavor you prefer): pureed roasted garlic (see page 35) or pan-braised garlic (see page 78); a drizzle of balsamic vinegar; chopped fresh herbs; pureed broiled pepper (see page 35); pureed mango or peach (with a little balsamic vinegar).

 Per recipe quantity

Total fat (g)	2
Saturated fat (g)	1
Unsaturated fat (g)	1
Cholesterol (mg)	6
Sodium (mg)	641
Calories	369

Makes
2½ cups (600ml)

VINAIGRETTE BASE

This mixture, based on balsamic vinegar and citrus juices with slivered black olives to give the unique flavor of olive oil, forms the base for countless no-oil vinaigrettes. It will keep for a week in the refrigerator.

INGREDIENTS

½ cup (125ml) balsamic vinegar

½ cup (125ml) lime juice

½ cup (125ml) orange juice

2 garlic cloves, crushed

3 black olives, slivered off their pits

1 tbsp Dijon mustard, or Red Pepper and Garlic Provençal mustard

pinch of sugar

Mix all the ingredients together in a screw-top jar, put on the lid, and shake well. Store in the refrigerator until needed.

VARIATIONS

Sun-Dried Tomato Vinaigrette: mix 2 tablespoons of the vinaigrette base with ⅓ cup (90ml) water and 2 sun-dried tomatoes and simmer until the tomatoes are plump and the liquid has almost evaporated. Put into a blender with the remaining vinaigrette base and process until smooth.

Mango Vinaigrette: put a quarter of the flesh of a large mango in a blender with the vinaigrette base and process until well mixed.

Broiled Pepper Vinaigrette: put ½ broiled pepper (see page 35) or ½ canned or jarred pepper, drained, in a blender. Add 1 quantity of the vinaigrette base and blend the mixture until smooth.

Beet Vinaigrette: chop half of a whole roasted beet (see page 78). Put in a blender with 1 quantity of the vinaigrette base and process until smooth.

Pear Vinaigrette: peel and dice half a juicy, ripe pear. Put in a blender with 1 quantity of the vinaigrette base and process until the mixture is smooth.

 Per recipe quantity

Total fat (g)	2
Saturated fat (g)	neg
Unsaturated fat (g)	2
Cholesterol (mg)	0
Sodium (mg)	684
Calories	95

Makes
1¼ cups (300ml)

SAUCES & SALSAS

A GOOD COLLECTION OF SAUCES used to include all of the classic emulsion sauces such as hollandaise, béarnaise, and beurre blanc, roux-based white sauces, olive oil-heavy tomato sauces – in fact, a catalog of high-fat techniques. But times change. Vegetable sauces and flavor infusions deliver texture and taste,

salsas – jeweled clusters of fresh and vibrant vegetables and fruits – provide verve. And how exciting it is to indulge in that most modern of pastimes, the mixing of culinary metaphors. Why *not* a Chinese/Mexican salsa or a Thai/Italian tomato sauce? Decide for yourself with these recipes.

TORTILLAS LAYERED WITH SALSAS
combine color and flavor in extravagant style.

USING SALSAS

The tortilla stack opposite is an imaginative mix of several recipes. From the top, the fillings are Mango & Fennel Salsa (see below), a layer of chargrilled peppers, Cherry Tomato & Red Onion Salsa (see below), Green Pea Guacamole (see page 50), Silky Stir-Fried Pepper Strips (see page 71), and Grilled Eggplant & Zucchini (see page 81).

CHERRY TOMATO & RED ONION SALSA

GREEN PEA GUACAMOLE

MANGO & FENNEL SALSA

CHERRY TOMATO & RED ONION SALSA

This very simple salsa includes wedges of ripe tomatoes rather than tomato pulp, giving it an interesting texture. It makes a colorful garnish: try it with Grilled Eggplant & Zucchini (see page 81), for instance.

INGREDIENTS

1 garlic clove, crushed

1 tbsp lime juice

juice of ½ orange

1 tbsp lemon juice

½ red onion, diced

1 tbsp balsamic vinegar

8 vine-ripened tomatoes

2 scallions, sliced

1 tbsp each chopped fresh parsley, mint, and cilantro

salt

1 Put the garlic, citrus juices, red onion, and balsamic vinegar in a large bowl, mix well, and let stand for 15–30 minutes.

2 Cut the tomatoes into quarters or eighths (depending on size) and add to the bowl. Sprinkle with the scallions and herbs. Season with a little salt and toss gently with two spoons until combined.

 Per serving

Total fat (g)	<1
Saturated fat (g)	neg
Unsaturated fat (g)	neg
Cholesterol (mg)	0
Sodium (mg)	42
Calories	23

Makes
6 servings

MANGO & FENNEL SALSA

The distinctively different yet complementary flavors of mango and fennel make this salsa memorable. It makes an excellent accompaniment for meats, particularly pork and poultry.

INGREDIENTS

1 tbsp balsamic vinegar

1 tbsp lime juice

1 garlic clove, crushed

1 red chili, seeded and finely chopped

1 mango, diced (see page 136)

1 head fennel, trimmed and diced, feathery fronds reserved and snipped

½ cucumber, peeled, seeded, and diced

1 small red onion, diced

3 scallions, sliced

2–3 tbsp each chopped fresh cilantro and flat-leaf parsley

2–3 tbsp shredded fresh mint

1 Put the balsamic vinegar, lime juice, garlic clove, and chili in a bowl, mix well, and marinate for 10–15 minutes.

2 Add the mango, the fennel (with a scattering of snipped fennel fronds), the cucumber, onions, and herbs. Mix with two spoons, gently tossing together all the ingredients.

 Per serving

Total fat (g)	<1
Saturated fat (g)	neg
Unsaturated fat (g)	neg
Cholesterol (mg)	0
Sodium (mg)	7
Calories	53

Makes
6 servings

BOLOGNESE SAUCE

Although this is not a real Bolognese Sauce (as soon as you eliminate the added fat, you break all the rules of traditional cooking), it is a deeply satisfying, meaty sauce with lots of flavor, thanks to the eggplant infusion. It's wonderful with tagliatelle or linguine, but it works well with pastas like lasagna or cannelloni too.

INGREDIENTS

2 eggplants, each about ¾lb (375g), trimmed, peeled, and diced (see pages 36–37)

2 red onions, chopped

2 garlic cloves, crushed

3 sun-dried tomatoes, chopped

pinch or 2 of crushed red pepper flakes (optional)

3 black olives, slivered off their pits

approximately 1¼ cups (300ml) stock (see page 30), plus extra as needed

4 tbsp dry red wine

1lb (500g) extra-lean ground meat (pork or beef)

two 14oz (425g) cans chopped tomatoes

salt and freshly ground black pepper

1 In a heavy-bottomed skillet, combine all the ingredients up to the meat. Cover and simmer briskly for 5–7 minutes. Uncover and cook, stirring occasionally, until the eggplant is very tender and the liquid is absorbed, adding a little more stock if needed. Remove from the heat, let cool slightly, then puree in a food processor or blender.

2 Meanwhile, sauté the meat in a nonstick skillet, breaking it up with a wooden spoon. Drain off any fat. Combine the meat and eggplant mixture in the skillet, add the tomatoes, with their juice, and season to taste. Simmer briskly, uncovered, for about 10 minutes, until thickened.

Per recipe quantity

Total fat (g)	25
Saturated fat (g)	8
Unsaturated fat (g)	15
Cholesterol (mg)	300
Sodium (mg)	1157
Calories	1049

Makes
6¼ cups (1.5 liters)

TOMATO EGGPLANT SAUCE

This combination of tomatoes and eggplant, enhanced by an almost Indian mix of spices and lemon juice, makes a rich, smooth, complex sauce that is excellent with pasta or as a bed for fish fillets.

INGREDIENTS

2 eggplants, peeled and chopped

2 red onions, chopped

8 garlic cloves, crushed and peeled

4 black olives, slivered off their pits

¼–½ tsp crushed red pepper flakes, to taste

1 tbsp ground cumin

1 tbsp ground coriander

2 tsp ground paprika

1 tsp ground turmeric

pinch of sugar, plus extra to taste

2 tbsp lemon juice, plus extra to taste

¾ cup (175ml) dry red wine

1¼ cups (300ml) stock (see page 30)

four 14oz (425g) cans chopped tomatoes

salt and freshly ground black pepper

2–3 tbsp fresh herbs such as cilantro, flat-leaf parsley, or mint, chopped or shredded

1 Combine in a wok or skillet all the ingredients except the tomatoes, seasoning, and herbs. Cover and simmer briskly for 7–10 minutes, then uncover and simmer until the eggplant and onions are meltingly tender and the liquid is absorbed.

2 Add the tomatoes and salt and pepper. Simmer, partially covered, for 15–20 minutes, until thickened. Let cool slightly.

3 Using a blender, puree the sauce in small batches until velvety smooth. The sauce may be prepared up to this point, then refrigerated or frozen.

4 When ready to use, bring the sauce to a simmer. Taste, and add seasoning or more lemon juice or a further pinch of sugar, as needed. Stir in the herbs and simmer for 5 minutes more.

Per recipe quantity

Total fat (g)	11
Saturated fat (g)	2
Unsaturated fat (g)	8
Cholesterol (mg)	0
Sodium (mg)	1250
Calories	590

Makes
9 cups (2 liters)

BOLOGNESE SAUCE

SICILIAN
VEGETABLE SALSA

TOMATO
EGGPLANT SAUCE

BASIL PESTO

SICILIAN VEGETABLE SALSA

This splendidly herby vegetable stew is based on the Arabian-influenced sweet and sour vegetable preserves of Sicily (with a few olives standing in for olive oil). It is a good accompaniment for Lemon-Garlic Roasted Chicken (see page 84) or Crusty Broiled Pork Cutlets (see page 95).

INGREDIENTS

1 zucchini, coarsely chopped

1 red onion, coarsely chopped

2 garlic cloves, crushed and peeled

1 chili, chopped

4 sun-dried tomatoes, chopped

4 black olives, slivered off their pits

1 tbsp capers, drained

2 tbsp golden raisins

1 head fennel, trimmed and coarsely chopped

1 red pepper, peeled and seeded (see pages 34–35)

1 tbsp balsamic vinegar

4 tbsp lemon juice, plus extra to taste

juice of ½ orange

slivered rind of ¼ lemon

salt and freshly ground black pepper

4 tomatoes, peeled, seeded, and cut into strips

1 tbsp chopped fresh flat-leaf parsley

½ tbsp chopped fresh oregano

1 tbsp torn fresh basil leaves

1 Combine all the ingredients except the tomato strips and herbs in a wok. Simmer, stirring occasionally; until the vegetables are just tender and the liquid is greatly reduced.

2 Stir in the tomato strips and simmer for 5–10 minutes, until the mixture is thick and the tomatoes have broken down. Taste, and add more seasonings and lemon juice, if desired.

3 Let cool slightly, then stir in the herbs. Serve as a main course with an accompanying mound of Garlic and Lemon Roasted Potatoes (see page 74), or as a first course with crusty bread.

 Per serving

Total fat (g)	<1
Saturated fat (g)	neg
Unsaturated fat (g)	<1
Cholesterol (mg)	0
Sodium (mg)	76
Calories	55

Makes
3¾ cups (900ml)
(6 servings)

WHITE PESTO

White Pesto is a creamy garlic spread – dynamite on crusty bread, but also good folded into freshly cooked pasta shapes such as penne.

INGREDIENTS

7oz (200g) Quark (if unavailable, use 7oz (200g) ricotta)

2 tbsp (30g) pine nuts

½ cup (75g) freshly grated Parmesan

about 12 cloves of Pan-Braised Garlic (see page 78)

Puree all the ingredients together in a food processor or blender

until smooth. Cover with plastic wrap and store in the refrigerator until ready to use.

VARIATION

For Creamy Basil Pesto, add a few handfuls of fresh basil and flat-leaf parsley before processing.

 Per recipe quantity

Total fat (g)	45
Saturated fat (g)	17
Unsaturated fat (g)	26
Cholesterol (mg)	77
Sodium (mg)	908
Calories	705

Makes
1¼ cups (300ml)

PEPPER SAUCE

There are many possibilities for jewel-colored sauces, using red or yellow peppers. I like to use sauces of both colors as a bed for fish, poultry, broiled eggplant and zucchini, and broiled meat.

INGREDIENTS

10 yellow or red peppers, unpeeled and coarsely chopped

2 garlic cloves, crushed

6 scallions, trimmed and sliced

1 chili, seeded and diced (optional)

½ tbsp paprika (with red peppers only)

1¼ cups (300ml) stock (see page 30)

salt and freshly ground black pepper

1 Put all the ingredients except the salt and pepper in a heavy-bottomed skillet. Bring to a boil, then reduce the heat and simmer for 20–30 minutes, until the vegetables are tender.

2 Season with salt and pepper. Let cool slightly.

3 Puree the mixture in batches in a food processor or blender. Strain through a sieve or strainer, rubbing the mixture through with a wooden spoon. Discard the tough skins left behind in the sieve.

4 Return the sauce to the pan and simmer until it is thick enough to coat the back of a spoon. Taste and adjust the seasoning, if necessary.

Per recipe quantity

Total fat (g)	4
Saturated fat (g)	1
Unsaturated fat (g)	2
Cholesterol (mg)	0
Sodium (mg)	319
Calories	371

Makes
3¾ cups (900ml)

TOMATO, GARLIC & PEPPER SAUCE

This is an interesting variation of homemade tomato sauce, rich with simmered garlic and pureed pepper, piquant and fragrant with chilies and lime juice. It makes a glorious pasta sauce, but it is even better under broiled meat, poultry, or fish.

INGREDIENTS

2 red onions, roughly chopped

8 garlic cloves, lightly crushed

4 sun-dried tomatoes, chopped

4 black olives, slivered off their pits

1lb (500g) red peppers, peeled, seeded, and roughly chopped (see page 34)

1 tsp ground cumin

½ tsp ground coriander

pinch or two of crushed red pepper flakes

1¼ cups (300ml) vegetable stock (see page 30), plus extra as needed

1¼ cups (300ml) dry red wine

four 14oz (425g) cans chopped tomatoes, or 3½lb (1.75kg) fresh tomatoes, peeled, seeded, and diced

salt and freshly ground black pepper

pinch of sugar (optional)

juice of 1 lime

chopped fresh herbs, to garnish

1 Put all the ingredients, up to and including the red wine, in a wok or heavy-bottomed saucepan. Cover, bring to a boil, and simmer briskly for 10 minutes.

2 Uncover and continue to simmer for a few minutes until the garlic, onions, and peppers are tender and the liquid is greatly reduced. Make sure the mixture remains moist: add a little more liquid if needed. When tender, the vegetables should be cooking in their own juices.

3 Stir in the tomatoes, salt and pepper, and a pinch of sugar if the tomatoes are particularly acidic. Simmer for 10–15 minutes, until thickened. Add the lime juice and more seasoning, as needed.

4 Pour the mixture into a blender and blend to a puree. Check the seasoning once more.

5 Add plenty of chopped fresh herbs, either leaving them as a garnish on top of the sauce or stirring them into it.

Per recipe quantity

Total fat (g)	8
Saturated fat (g)	1
Unsaturated fat (g)	5
Cholesterol (mg)	0
Sodium (mg)	1256
Calories	651

Makes
9 cups (2 liters)

Broiled Pepper & Oregano Pistou

This is a vivid, coarse pepper puree to be used by the dollop, as a garnish for soups and stews. It adds great visual pizzazz as well as a jolt of flavor.

Ingredients

2 large peppers, broiled, peeled, and diced (see page 35)

2–3 cloves Pan-Braised Garlic (see page 78)

2 tbsp fresh oregano leaves

1 tbsp chopped fresh flat-leaf parsley

½–1 tsp Sambal Oelek (Indonesian hot chili paste), to taste

2–3 tbsp freshly grated Parmesan

1 Combine all the ingredients in a food processor and process to a coarse puree.

2 Cover with plastic wrap and refrigerate. This sauce can be stored for several days.

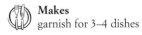

Per recipe quantity

Total fat (g)	14
Saturated fat (g)	8
Unsaturated fat (g)	6
Cholesterol (mg)	37
Sodium (mg)	485
Calories	312

Makes
garnish for 3–4 dishes

Roasted Vegetable Salsa

This salsa makes a fabulous dip with Pita Crisps (see page 53), fat-free potato chips, oven-fried potato wedges, oven-fried potato skins, or fat-free tortilla chips. It also makes a colorful and tempting garnish for many dishes in this book, including Crusty Broiled Pork Cutlets (see page 95) and Spicy Citrus-Scented Mexican Sausages (see page 94).

Ingredients

2 eggplants, each about ½lb (250g)

1 large head garlic, plus 2 garlic cloves, crushed

2 red peppers, broiled, peeled, and diced (see page 35)

1 chili, seeded and chopped

1 small red onion, chopped

2 sun-dried tomatoes, finely chopped

1 tbsp each lemon, orange, and lime juice

1 tbsp balsamic vinegar

4 ripe tomatoes, peeled, seeded, and diced

4 scallions, halved lengthwise and thinly sliced

6 tbsp chopped fresh flat-leaf parsley

4 tbsp torn fresh mint leaves

salt and freshly ground black pepper

1 Prick the eggplants in several places with a fork or thin skewer. Remove the papery outer covering of the whole head of garlic, but do not separate the cloves. Wrap the garlic in foil.

2 Bake the eggplants and garlic directly on the oven shelf of a preheated oven for 45–55 minutes, until the eggplant is soft and collapsed and the garlic is tender inside. Remove from the oven and put on a wire rack to cool.

3 Meanwhile, put the diced peppers, 2 crushed garlic cloves, chili, red onion, sun-dried tomatoes, citrus juices, and vinegar in a bowl and let marinate.

4 When the eggplants and garlic are cool enough to handle, remove and discard the stem and skin from the eggplants. Chop the flesh roughly and scrape into a food processor bowl.

5 Separate the roasted garlic cloves and squeeze each one over the bowl so that the pureed garlic pops out.

6 Add the remaining ingredients and the vegetables with their marinade. Season with salt and pepper and process to a rough puree.

Per serving

Total fat (g)	1
Saturated fat (g)	neg
Unsaturated fat (g)	1
Cholesterol (mg)	0
Sodium (mg)	15
Calories	68

Oven temperature
375°F/190°C

Cooking time
45–55 minutes

Makes
2½ cups (600ml) or 4 servings

TOMATO SAUCE

The secret of a good very low-fat tomato sauce is in the flavor infusion: it guarantees richness and depth. It is worth making the sauce in large quantities and then freezing it in batches. With a sauce like this on hand, all sorts of glorious meals are possible.

INGREDIENTS

2 red onions, chopped

4 sun-dried tomatoes, chopped

4 black olives, slivered off their pits

pinch or two of crushed red pepper flakes, to taste

4 garlic cloves, crushed

¾ cup (175ml) stock (see page 30)

¾ cup (175ml) red wine

four 14oz (425g) cans chopped tomatoes

pinch of sugar (optional)

salt and freshly ground black pepper

1–2 tbsp tomato paste

3 tbsp fresh herbs such as chopped flat-leaf parsley, oregano, or shredded basil

1 Put the onions, sun-dried tomatoes, olives, crushed pepper flakes, garlic, stock, and wine in a wok or skillet. Cover and simmer briskly for 5–7 minutes, then uncover and simmer until the onions are tender and the liquid is almost evaporated.

2 Stir in the chopped tomatoes and their juice and sugar, if the tomatoes are very acidic. Season with salt and pepper and simmer, partially covered, for 15–20 minutes.

3 Stir in the tomato paste and simmer for 5–10 minutes more. The sauce may be prepared up to this point, then chilled for several days or frozen.

4 When ready to serve, bring the sauce to a simmer and stir in the herbs. Check the seasoning and add more salt and pepper, if needed. Simmer for 5 minutes, then serve.

VARIATION

Arrabiatta Sauce: increase the garlic cloves to 8–10 according to your taste, and substitute 1–2 chopped chilies for the crushed red pepper flakes.

Per recipe quantity

Total fat (g)	5
Saturated fat (g)	1
Unsaturated fat (g)	3
Cholesterol (mg)	0
Sodium (mg)	1176
Calories	464

Makes
4½ cups (1 liter)

BLACK BEAN TOMATO SAUCE

Use ingredients from the pantry to whip together this Asian-inspired sauce. Serve the sauce to great effect with fish steaks or fillets, pork tenderloin, or broiled duck breasts.

INGREDIENTS

4 garlic cloves, peeled

1in (2.5cm) piece of fresh ginger

6–7 scallions, trimmed and chopped

1¼ cups (300ml) stock (see page 30)

¼ cup (60ml) dry sherry

1 tbsp oyster sauce

1 tsp Chinese chili sauce

2 tbsp Chinese black bean sauce

½ cup (125ml) passata

juice of 1 lime

2 tbsp chopped fresh cilantro

1 Crush together the garlic cloves and the ginger and put in a wok with the chopped scallions, stock, and sherry. Simmer briskly until the liquid has almost evaporated.

2 Stir in the oyster, chili, and black bean sauces and bring to a boil. Continue to boil, stirring, for a few seconds.

3 Stir in the passata, and then simmer briskly for 30 seconds. Stir in the lime juice and chopped cilantro and simmer for a few seconds longer.

Per recipe quantity

Total fat (g)	2
Saturated fat (g)	1
Unsaturated fat (g)	1
Cholesterol (mg)	0
Sodium (mg)	2082
Calories	199

Makes
1¼ cups (300ml)

CHINESE TOMATO SALSA

Wed a chunky Mexican salsa to Chinese seasonings for an explosion of flavor. This nontraditional salsa is a terrific accompaniment for fish, pasta, and meatballs.

INGREDIENTS

2 garlic cloves, crushed

1in (2.5cm) piece of fresh ginger, peeled and crushed

3 tbsp rice vinegar

¾lb (375g) cherry tomatoes

6 scallions, trimmed and chopped

2–3 tbsp chopped fresh cilantro

1 tsp sugar

1 tsp Chinese chili sauce

1 Put the crushed garlic and ginger and the rice vinegar in a bowl large enough to hold the whole salsa and let marinate for about 30 minutes.

2 Cut the cherry tomatoes into halves or quarters and add them with the scallions, cilantro, sugar, and Chinese chili sauce to the marinated ingredients. Mix everything together thoroughly before using.

Per serving

Total fat (g)	<1
Saturated fat (g)	neg
Unsaturated fat (g)	<1
Cholesterol (mg)	0
Sodium (mg)	50
Calories	30

Makes
1¼ cups (300ml) or 4 servings

WHITE BEAN, ORANGE & TARRAGON PUREE

I like this dolloped onto servings of soups or vegetable purees, but it works as a dip or spread as well. Change the herbs to your taste; if you don't like tarragon, try flat-leaf parsley or mint instead.

INGREDIENTS

14oz (425g) canned cannellini beans, drained and rinsed

1½ tbsp snipped fresh tarragon

1 tbsp Red Pepper Garlic Mustard

½ tbsp tomato paste

4–5 cloves Pan-Braised Garlic (see page 78)

juice of ½ large orange

2 tbsp lemon juice, plus extra to taste

dash or two of Tabasco sauce

salt and freshly ground black pepper

Puree all of the ingredients together in a food processor or blender. Taste, and add more citrus juices, Tabasco sauce, and salt and pepper, according to personal preference.

Per recipe quantity

Total fat (g)	4
Saturated fat (g)	1
Unsaturated fat (g)	3
Cholesterol (mg)	0
Sodium (mg)	2150
Calories	370

Makes
1¼ cups (300ml)

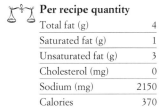

WHITE BEAN, ORANGE & TARRAGON PUREE

TOMATO SAUCE

BLACK BEAN TOMATO SAUCE

VEGETABLES

VEGETABLES LIE AT THE HEART of a healthy low-fat lifestyle. They make food beautiful to look at and delicious to eat. And, of course, they are life-enhancingly nutritious. Enrich your menus with an exciting mix of main-course vegetable dishes and vegetable accompaniments. Why not plan all-vegetable meals once in a while, mixing and matching several recipes from this collection? A beautifully coordinated feast of vegetables is the fresh, modern way to create a meal.

CAULIFLOWER STIR-FRIED IN RED WINE
takes on a sunset-pink color as well as a rich flavor as it cooks.

A FLAVOR INFUSION FOR STIR-FRYING

The flavor infusion for this recipe, made up of fresh chili, garlic, olives, sun-dried tomatoes, and onion, with wine and stock providing the liquid, needs only a short initial simmering before the main ingredients are added.

VEGETABLE STOCK

DRY RED WINE

RED ONION

RED CHILI

GARLIC

BLACK OLIVES

SUN-DRIED TOMATOES

CAULIFLOWER STIR-FRIED IN RED WINE

INGREDIENTS

4 black olives, slivered off their pits

4 sun-dried tomatoes, chopped

1 large red onion, cut into wedges

pinch of dried chili flakes, or more to taste

4 large garlic cloves, crushed

⅔ cup (150ml) dry red wine

1¼ cups (300ml) stock (see page 30)

4 red peppers, broiled, seeded, peeled,(see page 35) and cut into ½in (1cm) strips

2 heads of cauliflower, broken into florets

salt and freshly ground black pepper

4 tbsp lemon juice

chopped fresh flat-leaf parsley or oregano, to garnish

1 Put the olive pieces, sun-dried tomatoes, onion wedges, chili flakes, garlic, red wine, and ⅔ cup (150ml) of stock in a nonstick wok. Cover the wok, bring to a boil, and simmer briskly for 5 minutes.

2 Uncover the wok and add the peppers. Stir and simmer briskly for 2–3 minutes.

3 Add the cauliflower florets and the remaining stock. Season with salt and pepper, cover, and simmer briskly for 5 minutes, stirring occasionally.

4 Uncover the wok, then sprinkle over approximately 2 tablespoons of lemon juice. Continue to simmer, uncovered, until the cauliflower is tender and the liquid has reduced by two thirds.

5 Taste, adding the remaining lemon juice and adjusting the seasoning, if needed. Sprinkle the fresh parsley or oregano and serve.

Per serving

Total fat (g)	3
Saturated fat (g)	1
Unsaturated fat (g)	2
Cholesterol (mg)	0
Sodium (mg)	167
Calories	173

Makes
4 servings

GLAZED FENNEL

Looking a little like bulbous celery, but with a distinctive haunting anise flavor, fennel is a vegetable to be cherished. Crunchy, raw fennel in a salad is a great pleasure; fennel stir-fried in stock and lemon until meltingly tender and glazed is memorable. Illustrated on pages 113 and 151.

INGREDIENTS

3 fennel bulbs, stalks and outer layer trimmed and fronds reserved

2 tbsp lemon juice

⅔–¾ cup (150–175ml) stock (see page 30)

salt and freshly ground black pepper

1 large orange, peeled and chopped

2 black Calamata olives, slivered off their pits

1 Cut the fennel bulbs in half lengthwise, then cut across into ½in (1cm) slices.

2 Put the fennel in a skillet or wok with the lemon juice and ½ cup (125ml) of stock. Season with salt and pepper and stir-fry over high heat until the fennel is tender, but not mushy, and glazed with the reduced stock. Add a little more stock as needed.

3 Snip the fennel fronds and stir them in with the orange pieces and the olives. Serve hot as an accompaniment, as a topping for grilled polenta squares, or as an omelet filling.

Per serving

Total fat (g)	<1
Saturated fat (g)	neg
Unsaturated fat (g)	<1
Cholesterol (mg)	0
Sodium (mg)	78
Calories	36

Makes
4 servings

SWEET & SOUR RED ONIONS

Red onion slices, gently braised in a sweet, sour, and spicy mixture of balsamic vinegar, Dijon mustard, and stock, make a great sandwich filling, a garnish for steak, or a topping for fish. Illustrated on pages 113 and 151.

INGREDIENTS

6 red onions, peeled and halved lengthwise

2 cups (475ml) stock (see page 30)

½ tsp Dijon mustard

1½ tbsp balsamic vinegar

1 tbsp sugar

2 garlic cloves, crushed

pinch of dried chili flakes

1 Cut the onion halves lengthwise into ½in (1cm) slices. Place in a skillet with the remaining ingredients over medium-high heat.

2 Bring the mixture to a boil, then reduce the heat, cover, and simmer, stirring occasionally, for about 10 minutes.

3 Remove the cover and continue to simmer, stirring frequently, until the onions are nicely glazed and tender, but still a little crunchy.

Per serving

Total fat (g)	1
Saturated fat (g)	neg
Unsaturated fat (g)	1
Cholesterol (mg)	0
Sodium (mg)	126
Calories	143

Makes
4 servings

SILKY STIR-FRIED SWEET PEPPER STRIPS

S tir-fried in stock or in a mixture of stock and wine, pepper strips have a tender suppleness, sweetness, and color that make them pure pleasure on the plate.

INGREDIENTS

6 red peppers, halved, cored, and seeded

¾ cup (175ml) stock (see page 30)

freshly ground black pepper

1 Cut each of the pepper halves into their natural sections, then peel each piece using a swivel-bladed vegetable peeler. Cut each piece into ½in (1cm) wide strips.

2 Put the peppers and the stock in a heavy-bottomed skillet and set over medium-high heat. Add the black pepper and bring to a boil.

3 Gently toss the peppers in the hot stock and continue to cook until the liquid has reduced by two thirds.

4 Turn down the heat slightly and sauté the peppers in their juices for a few minutes until they are very tender and a thick sauce has formed.

5 Serve as crostini, with the pepper strips and pan juices piled onto garlic-rubbed, toasted slices of rustic bread. This dish would also work well served as a garnish, as part of a platter of mixed antipasto, or as a vegetable accompaniment to fish.

Per serving

Total fat (g)	1
Saturated fat (g)	neg
Unsaturated fat (g)	1
Cholesterol (mg)	0
Sodium (mg)	48
Calories	79

Makes
4 servings

OVEN-FRIED POTATOES

All you need for the most wonderful oven-fried potatoes – wedges, sticks, slices, whatever you prefer – are unpeeled potatoes, either big baking potatoes or small new potatoes, oil-water spray, and a nonstick baking sheet. Cooked this way, potatoes are exquisite: crunchy on the outside, fluffy and tender within, with a glorious taste of potato not spoiled by rivulets of grease. They make fabulous snacks and nibbles, or a first course, especially when dipped in an interesting sauce.

INGREDIENTS

2 or 3 baking potatoes, each about 6oz (180g), scrubbed

oil-water spray (see page 29)

salt

1 Pat the potatoes dry with paper towels and cut into wedges, sticks, or slices.

2 Oil-water spray a nonstick baking sheet and arrange the potato pieces, well spaced, on it. Roast in a preheated oven for about 10 minutes.

3 Take the baking sheet from the oven, shake up the potatoes, and turn them over. Return them to the oven and bake for another 15 minutes or so, until the potatoes are golden brown and puffed up. Salt them lightly and serve to great acclaim.

VARIATIONS

Oven-Fried New Potatoes: scrub 1lb (500g) new potatoes, cut in half, and bake as in the main recipe. New potatoes may take a little longer, perhaps 15 minutes on the first side, 20 minutes on the second side.

Spicy Oven-Fries: for 1lb (500g) of cubed all-purpose potatoes or peeled and cubed sweet potatoes, stir a few drops of lemon or lime juice into 1½ tablespoons tomato puree. Add about 1½ teaspoons spice mixture – perhaps an Indian mixture, such as turmeric, garam masala, cumin, and coriander; or a Mexican one, such as paprika and chili powder; or simply a good curry powder. Toss the potato cubes in the mixture and bake as in the main recipe, turning the potato cubes several times.

 Per serving

Total fat (g)	<1
Saturated fat (g)	neg
Unsaturated fat (g)	<1
Cholesterol (mg)	0
Sodium (mg)	105
Calories	87

 Oven temperature
425°F/220°C

 Cooking time
About 25 minutes

Makes
4 servings

GARLIC MASHED POTATOES

To make the creamiest, richest-tasting, no-fat mashed potatoes imaginable, start with very well baked (not boiled) potatoes. Then just follow my recipe.

INGREDIENTS

3 baking potatoes, each about 10oz (300g), scrubbed

9–12 roasted or pan-braised garlic cloves (see pages 35 and 78)

3–4 tbsp warm stock (see page 30)

3–4 tbsp warm skim milk

salt and freshly ground black pepper

snipped fresh chives, optional

1 Pierce the potatoes in several places with a fork or skewer and set them on a rack in the center of a preheated oven. Bake for about 2 hours.

2 Hold the potatoes with an oven mitt and pierce an X on the top of each with a fork. Squeeze so that the flesh comes surging up through the crisp skin. Scoop the flesh into a bowl and mash with a fork. (Save the crunchy skins for a snack.)

3 Add the garlic cloves and mash thoroughly. Mix in the stock and milk, a tablespoon of each at a time, until the preferred texture is achieved. Season and then stir in chives, if desired.

VARIATION

Garlic-Parmesan Mashed Potatoes: follow the main recipe, but replace the stock and milk with 1–2 tablespoons very low-fat fromage frais and 2–3 tablespoons grated Parmesan cheese.

 Per serving

Total fat (g)	<1
Saturated fat (g)	neg
Unsaturated fat (g)	<1
Cholesterol (mg)	neg
Sodium (mg)	28
Calories	110

 Oven temperature
400°F/200°C

 Cooking time
About 2 hours

 Makes
4 servings

SWEET POTATO PANCAKES

This is a very turn-of-the-twentieth century recipe. The color is tropical orange, the texture is tender with crispy edges, and the seasoning is a Mexican-Caribbean blend. Serve these as a first course or light meal with a mango salsa, or accompanied by Lima Bean & Prosciutto Stew (see page 116). They are also good with Braised Chicken Mexican (see page 87).

INGREDIENTS

2 egg whites

½ tsp each ground ginger, ground coriander, turmeric, ground cumin, and paprika

¼ tsp ground cinnamon

several dashes of Tabasco sauce

salt and freshly ground black pepper

2 tbsp lemon juice

1 large red onion

1lb (500g) orange-fleshed sweet potatoes, peeled

½ cup (60g) flour

oil-water spray (see page 29)

1 Lightly beat the egg whites in a large bowl. Whisk in the spices, Tabasco, salt, pepper, and lemon juice. Set aside.

2 Coarsely grate the onion into a colander, then grate the sweet potato over the onion. Whisk the flour into the egg mixture. With your hands, squeeze the grated potato and onion to get rid of excess liquid, then add to the egg mixture. Toss together gently until well mixed.

3 Oil-spray two nonstick baking sheets and warm them in a preheated oven. Use a large spoon to scoop dollops of potato mixture onto the sheets. Flatten each mound with the back of a spoon, then moisten with oil-water spray.

4 Bake for 7–10 minutes. Turn, and spray again. Bake for 5–7 minutes more, then turn. Repeat once or twice until tender, with crisp brown edges. Serve hot, with lime wedges, if desired.

VARIATION

White Potato Pancakes: replace the sweet potato with white potatoes. Omit the spices. Add a pinch of nutmeg and a generous sprinkling of snipped chives. Garnish with fromage frais mixed with chopped chives and horseradish, and perhaps a little shredded smoked salmon.

Per serving

Total fat (g)	1
Saturated fat (g)	neg
Unsaturated fat (g)	1
Cholesterol (mg)	0
Sodium (mg)	67
Calories	126

Oven temperature
450°F/230°C

Baking time
25–30 minutes

Makes
6 servings

NEW POTATOES WITH LEMON & MINT

These potatoes are resonant with lemon and are perfect with any pan-sautéed or roasted meat or poultry. I love their deep flavor – it doesn't just sit on top of the potatoes, it permeates them. The torn mint leaves complement them perfectly.

INGREDIENTS

1lb (500g) small new potatoes, scrubbed and halved lengthwise

1¼ cups (300ml) stock (see page 30), plus a little extra, as needed

4 tbsp freshly squeezed lemon juice

several dashes of Tabasco sauce

salt and freshly ground black pepper

handful of torn mint leaves, to garnish

1 Put the potatoes, stock, 2 tablespoons of lemon juice, and the Tabasco in a heavy-bottomed, nonstick skillet. Season with salt and pepper. Bring to a boil, then cover and simmer briskly for 5–7 minutes. Uncover and simmer, stirring occasionally, until the potatoes are very tender and the liquid has reduced. Do not let them burn: add a little more stock, if necessary.

2 When the potatoes are tender and the liquid has evaporated, stir the mixture and cook for another minute or so, until the potatoes are lightly toasted and speckled with brown. Sprinkle with the remaining lemon juice and scatter the mint leaves.

Per serving

Total fat (g)	<1
Saturated fat (g)	neg
Unsaturated fat (g)	<1
Cholesterol (mg)	0
Sodium (mg)	88.5
Calories	102

Makes
4 servings

GARLIC & LEMON-ROASTED POTATOES

These potatoes are perfect with Lemon-Garlic Roasted Chicken (see page 84). Both offer no compromise in flavor, although they are very low fat. The potatoes and garlic absorb the flavors of the added ingredients. Illustrated opposite.

INGREDIENTS

1½lb (750g) small, waxy, oval potatoes, scrubbed but unpeeled

2 tbsp lemon juice

1 large, firm head of garlic, split into separate cloves

4 sun-dried tomatoes, quartered

4 black olives, slivered off their pits

4–5 dashes of Tabasco sauce

dash of Worcestershire sauce

dash of teriyaki sauce

4 tbsp stock (see page 30), plus extra, as needed

oil-water spray (see page 29)

chopped fresh parsley, to garnish

1 Cut the potatoes into halves lengthwise and spread them out in a shallow roasting pan with the remaining ingredients, except the oil-water spray and the chopped parsley.

2 Mist with oil-water spray, then transfer to a preheated oven and roast for approximately 30 minutes, stirring occasionally and adding small amounts of stock as needed to prevent the potatoes from burning.

3 When the potatoes are tender, speckled with charred patches, and the pan juices are thick and syrupy, remove from the oven, sprinkle with chopped parsley, and serve.

VARIATION

This recipe is also delicious made with small whole new potatoes. Each tiny potato makes a succulent mouthful. Cooking time may be a little less.

 Per serving

Total fat (g)	<1
Saturated fat (g)	neg
Unsaturated fat (g)	<1
Cholesterol (mg)	0
Sodium (mg)	77
Calories	106

 Oven temperature
400°F/200°C

 Cooking time
About 30 minutes

 Makes
4 servings

MUSHROOMS MADE WILD

The "holy trinity" of fat-free mushroom cooking – stock, wine, and teriyaki sauce – brings out the mushroom flavor like nothing else. Add other flavor infusion ingredients and dried porcini, and your supermarket mushrooms will taste as if they were gathered in the woods at dawn. Illustrated on pages 113 and 151.

INGREDIENTS

4 garlic cloves, crushed

4 black olives, slivered off their pits

4 sun-dried tomatoes, chopped

1 chili, seeded and finely chopped

½ cup (125ml) dry red wine

1 cup (250ml) mushroom-soaking stock (see page 30)

1lb (500g) small mushrooms

½ cup (30g) dried porcini, soaked, rinsed, drained, and chopped

dash of teriyaki or soy sauce

1 Put the garlic, olives, sun-dried tomatoes, chili, wine, and half the stock in a heavy-bottomed, flat-bottomed wok or skillet. Bring to a boil and continue to boil until the liquid is reduced to approximately 1 tablespoon.

2 Add the mushrooms, the remaining mushroom stock, the rehydrated porcini, and the teriyaki or soy sauce to the pan.

3 Reduce the heat and simmer briskly, uncovered. Stir occasionally, until the mushrooms are tender and coated in the reduced sauce.

4 Serve the mushrooms heaped on grilled polenta squares (see page 113). They also make a delicious accompaniment to pork dishes.

 Per serving

Total fat (g)	1
Saturated fat (g)	neg
Unsaturated fat (g)	1
Cholesterol (mg)	0
Sodium (mg)	86
Calories	51

 Makes
4 servings

ARTICHOKES WITH AN HERBED OLIVE STUFFING

Artichokes stuffed with a savory bread mixture make a beautiful first course, served hot or cold, or part of an antipasto platter. When serving whole artichokes, remove the choke first, so that feasting on the stuffed thistle will be easy and stress-free. If you do not have artichoke stock on hand, vegetable stock will do nicely.

INGREDIENTS

6 artichokes, prepared to end of step 2 of Preparing Artichokes, opposite

½ cup (125ml) artichoke stock (see below), plus extra as needed

For the stuffing

2–3 large garlic cloves, crushed

1 tbsp balsamic vinegar

juice of ½ lemon

6 tbsp chopped fresh parsley

3 tbsp chopped fresh mint

1 cup (60g) day-old white bread, shredded

4–5 olives, slivered off their pits

1 tsp olive brine

freshly ground black pepper

3 tbsp artichoke stock

oil-water spray (see page 29)

1 Spread the artichokes' outer leaves apart, remove the cone of purplish leaves inside, and use a teaspoon to scrape out all the inedible hairy choke. Pour the stock into a shallow baking dish. Arrange the artichokes in one layer in the dish.

2 For the stuffing, put the garlic, vinegar, and lemon juice in a bowl, and let steep for 10 minutes.

3 Mix the parsley, mint, bread crumbs, olives, and olive brine together. Stir in the garlic mixture and grind black pepper over it to taste. Drizzle in the artichoke stock and mix everything together well.

4 Put a generous amount of stuffing into the center of each artichoke, slipping some of the stuffing down between the leaves. Sprinkle stock over each artichoke, then mist each one lightly with oil-water spray.

5 Loosely cover the artichokes with foil and bake in a preheated oven for 15 minutes. Remove the foil. If the stuffing looks dry, sprinkle with a little more stock and mist again with oil-water spray.

6 Return the artichokes to the oven for 10–15 minutes. Check for tenderness by piercing the bottom of an artichoke with the point of a knife. If it seems hard, return to the oven and bake for a few minutes longer.

VARIATIONS

Stuffed Artichoke Hearts: take 6 artichoke hearts (see Preparing Artichokes, opposite) and press about a tablespoon of the stuffing (above) on each. Arrange them in a single layer in a baking dish. Tuck the remaining stuffing over and around. Pour stock into the dish to a depth of 1in (2.5cm). Cover with foil and bake for 20–25 minutes. Uncover and sprinkle with 3 tablespoons Parmesan. Re-cover and bake for 20 minutes. Serve at once.

Artichokes with Vinaigrette: serve whole artichokes with Basic Vinaigrette (see page 59).

NOTE

Artichoke leaves make a vivid, intense stock. Put them in a large pan with plenty of cold water. Bring to a boil, then cover and simmer for about 45 minutes. Drain through a colander into a pan, then press down on the leaves to extract more liquid. Let cool, then pour into small containers and freeze. Artichoke stock makes a good base for soup, and is an excellent sauté medium.

Per serving

Total fat (g)	1
Saturated fat (g)	neg
Unsaturated fat (g)	1
Cholesterol (mg)	0
Sodium (mg)	161
Calories	68

Oven temperature
350°F/180°C

Cooking time
25–30 minutes

Makes
6 servings

ARTICHOKE & ZUCCHINI STIR-FRY

This stir-fry makes a vibrant first course, a light lunch, or a colorful accompaniment to fish or poultry – for example, grilled chicken breasts.

INGREDIENTS

6 baby zucchini

6 artichoke hearts (see Preparing Artichokes, below)

8 asparagus stalks

1 large red pepper

1 large yellow pepper

oil-water spray (see page 29)

approximately ½ cup (125ml) artichoke stock (see opposite) or other stock (see page 30)

salt and freshly ground black pepper

juice of ½ lime or lemon, to taste

1 Using a sharp knife, trim the zucchini and halve them lengthwise. Cut the artichoke hearts into strips.

2 Trim and peel the asparagus stalks, then cut them crosswise into 1in (2.5cm) lengths.

3 Peel the peppers (see page 34), halve, core, and seed them and cut them into strips.

4 Spray a nonstick, flat-bottomed wok with oil-water spray. Put the zucchini halves, artichoke strips, asparagus, and pepper strips into the wok.

5 Pour in the stock and season with salt and freshly ground black pepper.

6 Sauté over high heat, constantly stirring and turning the vegetables, until they are crisp but tender and the stock has reduced. Sprinkle with the lime or lemon juice.

7 Serve the stir-fry immediately, perhaps with slices of Wild Mushroom Bread (see page 146).

VARIATION

To make this a more substantial, non-vegetarian main dish, add slices of Smoked Spice-Rubbed Duck Breasts (see page 90), or serve it with Crusty "Grill-Fried" Pork Escalopes (see page 95).

Per serving

Total fat (g)	1
Saturated fat (g)	neg
Unsaturated fat (g)	<1
Cholesterol (mg)	0
Sodium (mg)	14
Calories	80

Makes
6 servings

PREPARING ARTICHOKES

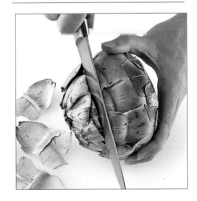

1 Cut or break off the stem of each artichoke, trim the base, and slice 1in (2.5cm) off the top. As soon as it is trimmed, drop each artichoke into a bowl of water acidulated with the juice of 1 lemon to prevent discoloration.

2 Snap off the artichoke's tough outer leaves. Put the whole artichoke into a pan of lightly salted boiling water and boil, partially covered, for 25–30 minutes. Drain, rinse under cold running water, and drain again, upside down.

3 To prepare artichoke hearts, pull off all the remaining leaves, reserving them for stock (see opposite). Pull out the purplish leaves over the heart. Using a paring knife and a teaspoon, scrape out all the inedible hairy choke.

4 When all vestiges of the inedible choke have been removed, trim the artichoke's hard base, leaving just the tender artichoke heart. It is now ready for stuffing and baking, or for using in dishes like the stir-fry above.

FENNEL

Fennel, the whole vegetable or its seeds, gives its anise blessing to several recipes in this book. Always trim the bulbs as described here before using in the chosen recipe.

To prepare whole fennel bulbs for cooking, trim away the tough outer layer and cut off the stalks and leaves from the head of the fennel bulb. (Save the trimmings for stock-making and the feathery fronds to use as an herb garnish.) Trim the bottom of the bulb slightly, but leave the core intact, since it helps keep the fennel sections together as they cook.

Per 1lb (500g)	
Total fat (g)	1
Saturated fat (g)	neg
Unsaturated fat (g)	1
Cholesterol (mg)	0
Sodium (mg)	55
Calories	60

OVEN-ROASTED BEETS

Acrid, flabby beets, overcooked and "preserved" with bad vinegar, debases the superb scarlet roots. Buy beets fresh, oven-roast them, and taste the difference.

Choose beets of a similar size, if possible. Wrap the prepared beets in heavy-duty foil (shiny side in). With smaller beets, wrap 2–3 in foil so that the beets are in roomy, well-sealed packages. Bake at 400°F (200°C) for 1–2 hours (the timing depends on the age and size of the beets). Use a skewer to test if the beets are tender. The skewer should go in easily, but the beets should not be mushy. Also, the skins will give slightly when pressed. Cool a bit, then slip off the skins.

Per 1lb (500g)	
Total fat (g)	<1
Saturated fat (g)	neg
Unsaturated fat (g)	<1
Cholesterol (mg)	0
Sodium (mg)	330
Calories	180

ASPARAGUS

Thick stalks of asparagus must be peeled, or they will turn fibrous when cooked. And cook them briefly: limp asparagus stalks are a scandal!

Unless the asparagus stalks are pencil-thin, peel them first to get maximum taste and texture out of the vegetable. Cut off the woody bottom of each stalk and use a swivel-bladed vegetable peeler to peel the stalk from the bottom end up to the bud. Rinse the stalks under cold running water and, if you are not going to use them at once, stand them in a glass of water as if they were a bunch of flowers, cover with a plastic bag, and keep in the refrigerator until needed.

To cook, put the stalks in a steamer basket and steam over boiling water for 3-7 minutes, depending on their size, until they are just tender. They should retain a hint of crispness. To test, hold up a stalk with tongs: it should bend just a little bit. If you intend to serve the asparagus hot, drain them on a clean dish towel set on a rack. If you plan to serve them cold, refresh them under cold running water to stop the cooking process and to set their bright green color. Drain and cool.

Per 1lb (500g)	
Total fat (g)	3
Saturated fat (g)	1
Unsaturated fat (g)	2
Cholesterol (mg)	0
Sodium (mg)	5
Calories	125

PAN-BRAISED GARLIC

Per 8oz (250g)	
Total fat (g)	2
Saturated fat (g)	1
Unsaturated fat (g)	1
Cholesterol (mg)	0
Sodium (mg)	280
Calories	296

Peel any number of garlic cloves (see page 35). Spread them out in a heavy-bottomed skillet and cover generously with stock. Cover tightly and simmer for 10–15 minutes, until the garlic cloves are meltingly tender and the stock is greatly reduced. (You may need to check and add some stock during cooking.) Drain the garlic (keep any leftover stock for soups or sauces) and puree, either by mashing it or pushing it through a fine-mesh nylon sieve.

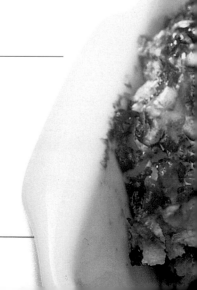

EGGPLANT & TOMATO GRATIN

Cooked in the traditional way, eggplant soaks up oil like an insatiable sponge. Save hundreds (maybe thousands!) of calories by broiling eggplant with a spritz of oil-water spray instead. As a result, this low-fat take on a beloved Italian home-cooking favorite will be ephemeral.

INGREDIENTS

10 heaping tbsp fresh white bread crumbs

5 tbsp freshly grated Parmesan cheese

salt and freshly ground black pepper

2 tbsp all-purpose flour

3 egg whites

2–3 dashes of Tabasco sauce

two ½lb (250g) eggplants, trimmed and peeled (see page 36)

oil-water spray (see page 29)

½ quantity Tomato, Garlic & Pepper Sauce (see page 64)

1 Put the bread crumbs in a shallow bowl with 3 tablespoons of Parmesan cheese. Season with salt and pepper.

2 Put the flour in another shallow bowl and season lightly with salt and pepper.

3 Put the egg whites in another shallow bowl and season with salt, pepper, and Tabasco. Beat lightly with a fork.

4 Preheat the broiler. Slice the eggplants on the diagonal, then dredge in the seasoned flour. Dip the slices on both sides into the egg whites and bread crumbs, then dip again in the egg and crumbs. Transfer the pieces to a platter as you work.

5 Spray a nonstick baking sheet with oil-water spray and place under the broiler to heat. Put the eggplant slices on the hot sheet and spray the tops.

6 Put under the hot broiler and broil, 4in (10cm) from the heat, for about 5 minutes, or until browned and sizzling. Loosen the slices carefully, turn, oil-spray, and broil on the other side for another 5 minutes, or until browned and tender. Meanwhile, heat the Tomato, Garlic & Pepper Sauce.

7 Lay the eggplant slices in a gratin dish and pour the sauce over the top. Sprinkle with the remaining Parmesan and place under the broiler until bubbly.

Per serving

Total fat (g)	6
Saturated fat (g)	3
Unsaturated fat (g)	3
Cholesterol (mg)	13
Sodium (mg)	403
Calories	208

Makes
6 servings

RICOTTA PARMESAN CUSTARD

This savory custard makes an exciting topping for Lasagna (see pages 110 and 111) and for vegetable dishes. For example, the Eggplant & Tomato Gratin (see page 79) can be topped with the custard instead of the Parmesan.

INGREDIENTS

3 egg whites

1 cup (250g) ricotta cheese

¼ cup (175ml) skim milk

5 tbsp freshly grated Parmesan

salt and freshly ground black pepper

1 Beat the egg whites with the ricotta, then beat in the milk and 4 tablespoons of Parmesan.

Season with salt and pepper. Pour the mixture over the chosen recipe, tilting the baking dish to produce an even coating.

2 Sprinkle the remaining Parmesan over the custard. Transfer to an oven preheated to 350°F/180°C. Bake for 30–40 minutes, until softly set and puffed and golden. Allow to sit for 5 minutes before serving.

 Per serving

Total fat (g)	9
Saturated fat (g)	6
Unsaturated fat (g)	3
Cholesterol (mg)	34
Sodium (mg)	222
Calories	132

 Makes
6 servings

BREADED EGGPLANT & ZUCCHINI SLICES

Serve these broiled vegetables (they look endearingly like fried fish) with Tomato, Garlic & Pepper Sauce (see page 64). They would also be good with a salsa from the Sauces & Salsas section, or with Basic Vinaigrette (see page 59) served as a dipping sauce.

INGREDIENTS

2 cups (500g) low-fat plain yogurt

1 red or yellow pepper, broiled, skinned, (see page 35) and pureed

1½ tsp Dijon mustard

5–6 tbsp fresh soft bread crumbs, from white or brown bread

4–5 tbsp freshly grated Parmesan

pinch or two of paprika

salt and freshly ground black pepper

1 eggplant, about ½lb (250g), peeled and trimmed (see page 36)

1 zucchini, about ⅓lb (180g), trimmed

oil-water spray (see page 29)

lemon wedges, to garnish

1 Put the yogurt in a bowl and gently whisk in the pepper puree and mustard. Pour onto a large plate and spread evenly.

2 Put the bread crumbs on another large plate, mix in the grated Parmesan and paprika, and season with salt and pepper. Spread out the mixture evenly.

3 Cut the eggplant and zucchini lengthwise into slices about ¼in (5mm) thick. Coat each slice with

the yogurt mixture, then dredge it in bread crumbs, pressing them on firmly.

4 Spray a nonstick baking sheet with oil-water spray and place it under a broiler to heat. When it is hot, take out from under the broiler and carefully spray again.

5 Arrange the eggplant and zucchini slices (in batches if necessary) on the sheet, leaving space around each one. Place 5in (12cm) below the broiler and cook for 3–5 minutes.

6 Remove the baking sheet from the heat and turn the slices over. Mist with oil-water spray and put back under the broiler until the reversed sides are browned and sizzling and the vegetable slices are very tender (check with the point of a knife or a skewer).

7 Transfer the cooked vegetable slices to a warm platter and keep warm while you broil the remaining slices.

8 Garnish the platter with lemon wedges and serve at once with your chosen sauce or salsa in a separate bowl.

 Per serving

Total fat (g)	8
Saturated fat (g)	4
Unsaturated fat (g)	3
Cholesterol (mg)	22
Sodium (mg)	494
Calories	259

 Makes
4 servings

GRILLED EGGPLANT & ZUCCHINI

The technique of twice-cooking zucchini and eggplant slices, first in an oil-water-sprayed skillet, and then in a ridged grill pan, ensures that the vegetables are meltingly tender with an elusive sweet and smoky barbecue flavor. I like to serve these as part of an antipasto, piled onto a platter with lemon wedges. They also make a wonderful filling for lasagna or for sandwiches.

INGREDIENTS

oil-water spray (see page 29)

1 long eggplant, about ½lb (250g), peeled and trimmed (see page 36)

2 tender young zucchini, about ¼lb (125g) each, trimmed

1 Oil-water spray a heavy-bottomed nonstick pan and set it and a ridged grill pan over medium heat to warm through.

2 Meanwhile, cut the eggplant and zucchini lengthwise into ¼in (5mm) thick slices. Place the slices, in batches, in the nonstick pan, leaving space around each slice. Cook for a minute or two on each side until tender and just beginning to show brown speckles, misting with the oil-water spray after turning.

3 Remove the pan from the heat and immediately transfer the slices in batches to the grill pan, keeping them well spaced. Grill for a minute or so on each side without spraying until marked by the grill.

4 Transfer each batch to a warm platter and keep warm while you grill the remaining slices.

Per serving

Total fat (g)	1
Saturated fat (g)	neg
Unsaturated fat (g)	1
Cholesterol (mg)	0
Sodium (mg)	2
Calories	23

Makes
4 servings

SPICED GREEN BEANS WITH LIME

An Asian-inspired treatment for tiny green beans. This dish is good hot, cold, or at room temperature. Use as an accompaniment to fish or Tandoori-Style Chicken (see page 86).

INGREDIENTS

juice of ½ lime

1¼ cups (300ml) stock (see page 30)

½–1 chili, seeded and finely chopped

½ tsp ground turmeric

½ tsp ground coriander

pinch of sugar

2 garlic cloves, crushed

½in (1cm) piece of fresh ginger, crushed

1lb (500g) tiny green beans, trimmed

salt and freshly ground black pepper

1 Mix together the lime juice, half the stock, the chili, the spices, sugar, garlic, and ginger in a wok and simmer over high heat until almost all the liquid has evaporated.

2 Add the beans and the remaining stock and season with salt and pepper. Cover and simmer for 2–4 minutes. Uncover and simmer briskly for about 2 minutes more, stirring continuously, until just tender – the beans should remain bright green and be slightly crunchy.

Per serving

Total fat (g)	<1
Saturated fat (g)	neg
Unsaturated fat (g)	<1
Cholesterol (mg)	0
Sodium (mg)	67.5
Calories	45

Makes
4 servings

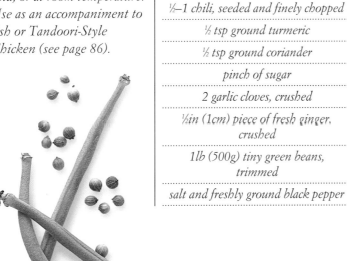

POULTRY

CHICKEN BREAST CUTLETS, without bones and skin, are delicate, low-fat morsels, but, alas, boringly bland. A whole roasted bird, minus its skin, fat, and the usual oily or buttery baste, can suffer the same insipid fate. Zap chicken cutlets with plenty of assertive herbs and spices, baste them in citrus juices and vegetable puree sauces, surround them with heady collections of vegetables, and they will take on deep character. Duck breasts and chicken thighs, stripped of skin and fat, are more robust in flavor, but also benefit from bold seasoning. Cook chicken thoroughly, but don't overcook it: *over*cooked means dry and stringy.

CHICKEN WITH MEDITERRANEAN VEGETABLES
looks beautiful served on a platter with lemon wedges and a lavish garnishing of fresh herbs.

MAKING A FLAVOR INFUSION

The flavor infusion for this dish is based on vegetables with a Mediterranean slant, including olives, peppers, and sun-dried tomatoes.

RED ONION

GARLIC CLOVES

SUN-DRIED TOMATO

BLACK OLIVES

EGGPLANT

RED AND YELLOW PEPPERS   RED CHILI

DRY WHITE WINE

CHICKEN STOCK

CAPERS

RAISINS

CHICKEN WITH MEDITERRANEAN VEGETABLES

INGREDIENTS

4 boned chicken breast halves

For the marinade

4 garlic cloves, crushed

2 olives, slivered off their pits

juice of 1 large orange

⅓ cup (90ml) lemon juice

2 tbsp balsamic vinegar

2 dashes of teriyaki sauce

For the vegetable flavor infusion

1 large red onion, halved and sliced

4 garlic cloves, crushed

4 sun-dried tomatoes, chopped

4 black olives, slivered off their pits

1 red chili, seeded and chopped

6oz (180g) eggplant, peeled and diced (see page 36)

2 tbsp each raisins and capers

1 red and 1 yellow pepper, seeded, peeled, and cut into strips

1¼ cups (300ml) stock (see page 30)

1¼ cups (300ml) dry white wine

salt and freshly ground black pepper

oil-water spray (see page 29)

1 Put the skinned and trimmed chicken breasts in a dish. Mix the marinade ingredients and pour over the chicken. Let steep.

2 Heat the flavor infusion ingredients in a skillet, cover, and simmer for 5–7 minutes. Uncover and simmer until the vegetables are tender.

3 Heat a ridged grill pan and spray with oil-water spray. Shake the marinade off the chicken and grill for 2–3 minutes on each side. Lay the chicken in one layer on the vegetables in the pan. Cover and simmer gently, turning, for 7–8 minutes until cooked. Garnish with fresh herbs, if desired.

Per serving

Total fat (g)	3
Saturated fat (g)	1
Unsaturated fat (g)	2
Cholesterol (mg)	84
Sodium (mg)	290
Calories	271

Makes
4 servings

LEMON-GARLIC ROASTED CHICKEN

I really feel that this is the ultimate roasted chicken. It proves triumphantly that very low-fat cooking does not mean compromising on flavor. Serve the succulent bird and its delicious natural gravy with Garlic and Lemon-Roasted Potatoes. As with all chicken recipes, while the bird should be at room temperature when it goes into the oven to ensure even cooking right through, never leave it sitting in a warm atmosphere before cooking it.

INGREDIENTS

1 large head garlic (about 14 large cloves), separated

4 sun-dried tomatoes, halved lengthwise, and 1 sun-dried tomato, chopped

4 black olives, slivered off their pits

2 cups (500ml) stock (see page 30)

several dashes of Tabasco sauce

1–2 dashes each of teriyaki and Worcestershire sauces

one 2½–3lb (1.25–1.5kg) chicken, trimmed of all fat

⅓ cup (90ml) lemon juice (lemon halves reserved)

1 lemon, thinly sliced and seeds removed

1 large onion, sliced

about ¾ cup (175ml) dry vermouth

salt and freshly ground black pepper

½–¾ cup (125–175ml) dry vermouth (for the gravy)

1 large bunch watercress, to garnish

1 Lightly crush 12 garlic cloves to loosen the skins. Remove the skins and halve each clove. Remove any central green sprouts.

2 Put the halved garlic in a skillet with the sun-dried tomato halves, olives, 1¼ cups (300ml) stock, Tabasco, teriyaki, and Worcestershire sauces. Simmer briskly until the garlic is very tender and the liquid is greatly reduced and syrupy. Allow to cool.

3 Make small incisions all over the chicken (except the breast). Rub lemon juice over the bird. Loosen the breast skin and rub lemon juice under the skin. Put the lemon halves into the main cavity.

4 Spread the lemon slices and garlic mixture evenly under the breast skin. Transfer to a glass or ceramic dish, cover, and chill for several hours or overnight.

5 Take the bird out of the refrigerator and tie its legs together. Scatter the onion, remaining garlic, chopped, and chopped sun-dried tomato in a roasting pan. Put a rack in the pan.

6 Pour ¼ cup (60ml) each of stock and vermouth into the pan. Season the chicken, roast it breastside down on the rack for 30 minutes, then roast it breastside up for about 40 minutes.

7 Add more stock and vermouth as needed to keep the juices plentiful, and baste the chicken occasionally. Turn it regularly to keep it from browning too much. It is done when golden brown and the juices run clear when the leg joint is pricked. Let it rest for 10 minutes, then remove the skin and flavor ingredients underneath it.

SERVING THE CHICKEN

1 For the gravy, pour the pan juices through a sieve into a bowl. Press down on the solids to squeeze out all the goodness. Discard the solids. Freeze the pan juices for 10 minutes, so that the fat can rise to the top and solidify.

2 Put the roasting pan on the burner, pour in the vermouth, and reduce the liquid by half, scraping up the browned deposits. Skim the fat from the chilled pan juices, pour the juices into the roasting pan, and bring to a boil. Pour into a warmed pitcher.

3 Garnish the carved chicken with watercress and serve with the gravy and Garlic and Lemon-Roasted Potatoes (see page 74).

Per serving

Total fat (g)	32
Saturated fat (g)	9
Unsaturated fat (g)	22
Cholesterol (mg)	226
Sodium (mg)	360
Calories	515

Oven temperature
450°F/230°C

Cooking time
About 1½ hours

Makes
4 servings

SMOKED ROSEMARY LEMON CORNISH HENS

In low-fat cooking, flavor is all. Cross-cultural French/Chinese overtones – a rosemary-garlic-olive-lemon mixture stuffed under the skin, and tea, sugar, and rice in the wok for smoking – imbue these birds with fabulous flavor. The Cornish hens are wok-smoked first, then oven-roasted. The roasting time depends on the force of the heat under the wok during the initial smoking, so treat the final roasting times given here as a guide only.

INGREDIENTS

2 Rock Cornish game hens, each about ¾lb (425g), fat trimmed

4 garlic cloves

6 black olives, slivered off their pits

4 tbsp fresh rosemary needles, plus 2 long sprigs

juice of 2 lemons

mixed peppercorns

3 rounded tbsp Lapsang Souchong tea or the contents of 6 teabags

3 rounded tbsp brown sugar

3 rounded tbsp white rice

salt

oil-water spray (see page 29)

1 Loosen the skin over the breasts and legs of the Cornish hens by running your finger between the skin and the flesh.

2 Crush together the garlic and olives and mix with the rosemary needles and half the lemon juice. Slip this mixture under the skin of the hens, pushing it over the breasts and down to the legs. Sprinkle the remaining lemon juice over the birds and grind over the peppercorns. Cover and marinate in the refrigerator for several hours or overnight.

3 Line a wok with a tight-fitting lid with aluminum foil, leaving an overhang around the edge (see Smoked Spice-rubbed Duck Breasts, page 90).

4 Spoon the tea, sugar, and rice onto the aluminum foil, then cut up the rosemary sprigs and add them as well. Put a steaming rack in the wok.

5 Season the Cornish hens with salt, then arrange them, breastside down, on the rack and cover the wok. Crimp the foil around the lid to prevent smoke from escaping. Turn the heat to high for 5 minutes, then cook on low for another 20 minutes. Meanwhile, preheat the oven and line a baking sheet with foil, shiny side up. Place a rack on the sheet.

6 Spray the rack with oil-water spray. Put the smoked hens, breastside up, on the rack and roast in the preheated oven for 10 minutes. Turn breast down and roast for 10 minutes. Finally, turn breast up again and cook for 5 minutes. Remove from the oven and let rest for 5 minutes.

7 To serve, strip off and discard the skin and the herb-garlic mixture, which will have permeated the flesh. Carve the Cornish hens and serve the pieces on warm plates. Alternatively, present each diner with half a bird, and let him or her tackle it (it's less elegant, but more rewarding).

Per serving	
Total fat (g)	21
Saturated fat (g)	6
Unsaturated fat (g)	14
Cholesterol (mg)	140
Sodium (mg)	215
Calories	420

Oven temperature
450°F/230°C

Cooking time
50 minutes

Makes
4 servings

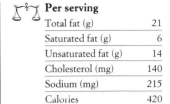

TANDOORI-STYLE CHICKEN

𝒲ithout a conical clay tandoor oven, there is no true tandoori chicken, so this is an approximation only – but a delicious one. A combination of grilling and roasting gives the right effect here.

INGREDIENTS

4 boned chicken breast halves, skinned and trimmed

salt and freshly ground black pepper

1 tbsp each ground coriander and ground cumin

1 tsp each ground turmeric and garam masala

¼ tsp each freshly grated nutmeg, ground cinnamon, chili powder, and ground cardamom

pinch of ground cloves

1½ cups (350ml) low-fat yogurt

6 garlic cloves, crushed

1in (2.5cm) piece of fresh root ginger, peeled and crushed

oil-water spray (see page 29)

chopped fresh cilantro leaves, to garnish

1 Pull the small, thin fillet from each chicken breast. Pierce each piece of chicken in several places with a thin skewer. Season with salt and pepper.

2 Mix the remaining ingredients except the oil-water spray and garnish. Toss the chicken in this mixture and spread out the pieces in a ceramic or glass baking dish.

Cover tightly with plastic wrap and chill in the refrigerator for several hours or overnight.

3 When ready to cook the chicken, oil-water spray a nonstick baking sheet and put it in the preheated oven.

4 Heat a ridged grill pan over a burner. When it is very hot, lay the chicken on the pan in a single layer and grill for 1½–2 minutes on each side, turning occasionally, until the pieces are well seared and striped with characteristic barbecue hatchmarks.

5 Transfer the larger seared cutlets to the baking sheet and cook in a preheated oven until just done, approximately 4–5 minutes, depending on size. They are done when they feel firm yet springy. The smaller pieces will cook through on the grill pan in 3–4 minutes.

6 Slice all the chicken pieces across the grain. Serve on a bed of fragrant rice, garnished with the cilantro. Accompany with lime wedges, pickles, chutney, and Herbed Raita (see page 52).

Per serving	
Total fat (g)	3
Saturated fat (g)	1
Unsaturated fat (g)	2
Cholesterol (mg)	86
Sodium (mg)	151
Calories	170

Oven temperature
450°F/230°C

Cooking time
about 7 minutes

Makes
4 servings

CHICKEN BREASTS WITH BRAISED PRUNES & SHALLOTS

Brandy-saturated prunes simmered with fresh tarragon, garlic, and shallots give chicken breasts great character. They give the chicken the deep, dark flavors I crave, and the colors are richly autumnal.

INGREDIENTS

4 boned chicken breast halves, skinned and well trimmed

salt and freshly ground black pepper

½ cup (125ml) dry white wine

2 tbsp brandy

½ cup (125ml) stock (see page 30)

6 prunes, pitted and quartered

oil–water spray (see page 29)

4 shallots, cut into eighths

2 garlic cloves, crushed

1½ tbsp chopped fresh tarragon

large bunch of watercress, to garnish

1 Season each chicken breast with a little salt and plenty of pepper. Put the wine, brandy, stock, and prunes in a bowl.

2 Spray a nonstick skillet liberally with oil-water spray, and heat until it sizzles. Add the chicken breasts, brown them for 1–2 minutes on each side, then set them aside.

3 Pour the wine mixture into the skillet, add the shallots, garlic, and 1 tablespoon of tarragon and bring to a boil. Boil rapidly, deglazing the pan by scraping up the deposits on the bottom.

4 When the shallots are tender and the liquid greatly reduced, return the chicken to the pan with the remaining tarragon. Cook for 2–3 minutes only, turning the cutlets until they are mahogany brown and just cooked through. Add a splash of stock and wine, if needed, but remember that the sauce should be thick and syrupy.

5 Arrange the chicken on a warm platter with the prune-shallot mixture. Garnish with the watercress and serve.

Per serving	
Total fat (g)	2
Saturated fat (g)	<1
Unsaturated fat (g)	1
Cholesterol (mg)	84
Sodium (mg)	104
Calories	178

Makes
4 servings

BRAISED CHICKEN MEXICAN

A Mexican-inspired dish in which the method of braising ensures that the seasoning infuses the chicken right down to the bone, and that the texture is deliciously succulent. Serve it with Sweet Potato Pancakes (see page 73) and Cherry Tomato & Red Onion Salsa (see page 61).

INGREDIENTS

3 garlic cloves, crushed

½ red and ½ green chili, seeded and chopped

12 scallions, trimmed and sliced

juice of 1 lime

grated zest of ½ lime

½ tbsp ground cumin

½ tsp ground coriander

1 tbsp dark rum

1 tbsp tomato paste

salt and freshly ground black pepper

6 chicken thighs, skinned and trimmed

1 cup (250ml) stock (see page 30)

chopped fresh cilantro leaves, to garnish

1 Put all the ingredients in a bowl except the chicken, stock, and cilantro. Toss the chicken in this mixture and marinate for up to 30 minutes.

2 Put the chicken thighs, with the marinade, in a single layer in a heavy-bottomed skillet. Pour in the stock.

3 Bring to a simmer. Continue to simmer for approximately 20 minutes, turning the chicken occasionally, until it is just done and the pan juices have cooked down to a thick, terracotta-colored sauce.

4 Sprinkle with cilantro and serve with lime wedges.

Per serving	
Total fat (g)	2
Saturated fat (g)	<1
Unsaturated fat (g)	1.5
Cholesterol (mg)	68
Sodium (mg)	125
Calories	97

Makes
4 servings

GRILLED CHICKEN WITH SWEET POTATO & LIME SAUCE

The sauce is a vivid blaze of yellow-orange and the chicken is exquisitely tender. For a change, prepare the recipe through the middle of step 3, but leave the vegetable mixture unpureed. Cube the grilled chicken and combine with the vegetables.

INGREDIENTS

juice of 1 lime

juice of ½ orange

½ tsp each turmeric, cumin, and coriander

salt and freshly ground black pepper

4 boneless, skinless chicken breasts

For the sauce

2–3 garlic cloves, crushed

1in (2.5cm) piece of fresh ginger, crushed

2 cardamom pods, lightly crushed

4 scallions, sliced

½ tsp each cumin, turmeric, and ground coriander

1lb (500g) orange-fleshed sweet potato, peeled and diced

1¼ cups (300ml) stock (see page 30)

juice and zest of ½ lime

few drops of lemon juice

chopped fresh cilantro, to garnish

1 Rub the juices, spices, and salt and pepper into the chicken. Marinate while making the sauce.

2 To make the sauce, sauté the garlic, ginger, cardamom, scallions, spices, and sweet potato in a covered pan for 7–10 minutes. Uncover and cook for 3–5 minutes, until the vegetables are tender. Discard the cardamom.

3 Add the stock, lime juice and zest, lemon juice, and salt and pepper. Process in a blender or food processor, then push through a sieve, discarding the solids.

4 Grill the chicken in a grill pan for 2–3 minutes, then finish in a preheated oven for 6–7 minutes. Reheat the sauce, taste, and adjust the seasoning. Spoon onto plates, put the chicken on the sauce, and garnish with the cilantro, and with spikes of chives, if desired.

Per serving

Total fat (g)	2
Saturated fat (g)	1
Unsaturated fat (g)	1
Cholesterol (mg)	84
Sodium (mg)	194
Calories	260

Oven temperature
425°F/220°C

Cooking time
18–25 minutes

Makes
4 servings

DUCK BREASTS WITH CRANBERRY CHUTNEY

The richness of duck breast is beautifully complemented by a sweet and sour chutney of plumped dried cranberries. The skinned duck – lean as can be – is cooked briefly so that it remains pink and succulent. Orange-Thyme Scented Wild Rice (see page 115) is the perfect accompaniment.

INGREDIENTS

4 boned duck breasts, skinned and trimmed of any fat

1 tbsp mixed peppercorns, crushed

oil-water spray (see page 29)

For the marinade

juice of ½ orange

4 tbsp lemon juice

½ tbsp balsamic vinegar

½ tbsp sweet vermouth

2 garlic cloves, crushed

½in (1cm) piece of fresh ginger, crushed

¼ tsp each ground turmeric, ground cumin, and ground coriander

For the chutney

½in (1cm) piece of fresh ginger, crushed

2 garlic cloves, crushed

1 red onion, chopped

1 chili, seeded and chopped

juice of ½ orange

4 tbsp lemon juice, plus extra (see method)

⅔ cup (150ml) stock (see page 30)

½ cup (125ml) sweet vermouth

1 tbsp balsamic vinegar

¼ cup (75g) dried cranberries

1 Coat the duck breasts on both sides with the crushed pepper and place them in a single layer in a glass or ceramic dish.

2 Mix together the marinade ingredients and pour the mixture over the duck. Turn the breasts in the liquid so that they are evenly coated. Marinate at room temperature for 1–2 hours, or for several hours in the refrigerator. If refrigerated, let them come to room temperature before continuing.

3 Meanwhile, put the chutney ingredients in a saucepan, bring gently to a boil, and simmer until the onions are tender, the cranberries are plump, and the liquid is reduced to a syrupy glaze. Taste, and add a little more lemon juice, if needed. Set aside.

4 Spread the chutney in a large flameproof, ovenproof skillet large enough to hold the duck pieces in a single layer and bring to a simmer.

5 Meanwhile, oil-water spray a heavy-bottomed nonstick skillet and heat it on a burner. Sear the marinated duck breasts in the skillet for about 1 minute on each side.

6 Set the duck on top of the chutney in a single layer and transfer the pan to a preheated oven. Roast for 7 minutes, until cooked, but still pink inside: the duck breasts should feel firm yet springy (not hard or mushy).

7 Set the duck on a chopping board and let rest for 5 minutes. Spread the chutney out on a serving plate. Slice the duck across the grain and arrange the slices, overlapping slightly, on the chutney. Drizzle on any meat juices that have gathered under the duck breasts. Serve immediately.

Per serving

Total fat (g)	6
Saturated fat (g)	2
Unsaturated fat (g)	4
Cholesterol (mg)	132
Sodium (mg)	178
Calories	241

 Oven temperature
400°F/200°C

Oven cooking time
7 minutes

Makes
4 servings

SMOKED SPICE-RUBBED DUCK BREASTS

A long time ago, my friend chef Frank Ma of Atlanta, Georgia, taught me how to smoke small pieces of poultry in a wok. It's a marvelous technique to apply to low-fat cooking, because the process leaves the poultry permeated with a haunting and compelling smokiness. Here I give three recipes using smoked duck breasts. Illustrated opposite is Duck and Pear Salad.

INGREDIENTS

3 rounded tbsp Lapsang Souchong tea, or the contents of 6 Lapsang Souchong tea bags

3 rounded tbsp white rice

3 rounded tbsp brown sugar

2–4 duck breasts, skinned and trimmed

good pinch or two each hot paprika, ground coriander, and ground cumin

freshly ground black pepper

juice of 1 lime

oil-water spray (see page 29)

1 Line a wok with a tight-fitting lid with aluminum foil, leaving an overhang. Sprinkle in the tea, rice, and brown sugar. Put a steamer or wire rack in the wok.

2 Put the duck breasts on a plate. Sprinkle with the spices and grind pepper evenly on both sides of the duck breasts. Rub the mixture in. Squeeze the lime juice over the breasts and turn them in the juice.

3 Put the duck pieces on the wire rack and cover. Crimp the foil around the lid to keep the smoke in. Turn the heat to high for 5 minutes, then down to low for 5 minutes. Remove from the heat and let sit, still covered, for 5 more minutes.

4 Oil-water spray a ridged grill pan and heat. Grill the duck breasts, turning once or twice and oil-water spraying them briefly. They are best kept rare, and may take anywhere from 2 minutes to 6 or 7, depending on their size, the heat, and your grill pan. Slice across the grain and serve with any pan juices.

VARIATION

Duck and Pear Salad: line a platter with watercress or arugula. Arrange slices of Smoked Duck Breasts, sliced pears, asparagus spears, and fresh raspberries or blueberries. Drizzle with Pear Vinaigrette (see page 59) and sprinkle with fresh herbs.

Per serving

Total fat (g)	6
Saturated fat (g)	2
Unsaturated fat (g)	4
Cholesterol (mg)	132
Sodium (mg)	132
Calories	151

Makes
2–4 servings

SMOKED DUCK FAJITAS

This is a smoky, sensual, spicy, convivial glory of a feast, centering around the wonderful spiced and smoked duck breasts of the recipe above. No one could feel glum sitting down to a meal like this.

INGREDIENTS

16–20 flour tortillas

4 Smoked Spice-Rubbed Duck Breasts (see above), sliced across the grain or cut into strips

selection of roasted vegetables, such as red and yellow peppers, zucchini, and eggplant

Green Pea Guacamole (see page 50)

Cherry Tomato & Red Onion Salsa (see page 61)

Mango & Fennel Salsa (see page 61)

Herbed Raita (see page 52)

1 Wrap the tortillas together in foil and warm in a preheated oven for 10 minutes.

2 Set the tortillas, duck breasts, and roasted vegetables on the table. Put the Guacamole, salsas, and Herbed Raita in separate dishes and arrange them around the tortillas, duck breasts, and vegetables. Encourage each diner to wrap various combinations of smoked duck and other dishes in the tortillas.

Oven temperature
350°F/180°C

Cooking time
10 minutes

Makes
4 servings

MEAT

RED MEAT HAS HAD SOMETHING of a bad press lately, but it is too nutritionally valuable to ignore entirely. The secret is to eat small amounts of lean meat only occasionally, and to surround and augment them with plenty of vegetables, grains, and fruit. I can never overemphasize the importance of vegetables: even when planning meat dishes, vegetables should figure prominently. In this section, meatballs and sausages, for instance, are lightened with eggplant; braised beef is bathed in a rich vegetable puree gravy; and roasted and sautéed meats share the billing with salsas, preserves, salads, and relishes.

CUBAN PORK WITH A MANGO SALSA
*combines flavorful marinating and fast
"grill-roasting" to ensure succulent meat,
bursting with juice.*

A SPICY SALSA TO SERVE WITH MEAT

Mango-Papaya Salsa served with Cuban Pork both enhances and contrasts with the flavor of the marinated meat. A chili (as hot as you like) and red onion give the salsa bite, and fruits and herbs contribute a mixture of more delicate flavors.

MINT

CILANTRO

CHILI

MANGO-PAPAYA SALSA

MANGO

PAPAYA

RED ONION

LIME JUICE

CUBAN PORK WITH A MANGO-PAPAYA SALSA

INGREDIENTS

1 pork tenderloin, about 1lb (500g), very well trimmed

For the marinade

½ cup (125ml) orange juice

3 tbsp lemon juice

1 cup (250ml) water

2 tbsp lime juice

½ head garlic, cloves crushed

2 tbsp soy sauce

freshly ground black pepper

2 tbsp dried oregano

4 bay leaves

For the Mango-Papaya Salsa

1 mango, diced (see page 136)

1 papaya, diced

1 small red onion, diced

3 tbsp lime juice

1 chili, seeded and chopped

2 tbsp chopped fresh cilantro

2 tbsp shredded fresh mint

1 Put the pork in a shallow glass dish. Mix together the marinade ingredients and pour over the pork. Leave for 30 minutes–24 hours, turning the meat in the marinade occasionally.

2 Line a roasting pan with foil and pour in water to a depth of ½in (1cm). Lightly oil-water spray a wire rack and put in the pan. Put the pork on the rack, reserving the marinade. Roast in a preheated oven for 20–25 minutes, turning it after 12 minutes and basting with the marinade.

3 While the meat is cooking, mix together the salsa ingredients to serve with the pork.

4 Remove the pork from the oven and let rest for 5–10 minutes. To serve, thinly slice across, slightly on the diagonal.

VARIATION

Korean Pork Marinade: 1 tbsp crushed fresh ginger, ½ head garlic, crushed, 1 bunch scallions, sliced, ½ cup (125g) sugar, ½ cup (125ml) teriyaki or soy sauce, 1 cup (250ml) water. Serve Korean Pork with an oriental dipping sauce.

Per serving	
Total fat (g)	5
Saturated fat (g)	2
Unsaturated fat (g)	3
Cholesterol (mg)	75
Sodium (mg)	171
Calories	234

Oven temperature
450°F/240°C

Cooking time
20–25 minutes

Makes
4 servings

SPICY, CITRUS-SCENTED MEXICAN SAUSAGES

The meat for these sausages is very, very lean, and the eggplant ensures it is succulent. Go for a gorgeous presentation for these characterful delicacies, serving them on tortillas and with rich sauces such as Tomato, Garlic & Pepper Sauce (see page 64) or Cherry Tomato & Red Onion Salsa (see page 61). If you prefer, replace the lean pork with turkey meat in all three recipes here.

INGREDIENTS

½lb (250g) extra-lean pork tenderloin, trimmed and ground

one ½lb (250g) eggplant, roasted, peeled, and chopped (see page 37)

2 scallions, chopped

3 cups (375g), plus 3 tbsp, fresh bread crumbs

1 tbsp chopped fresh parsley

1 tbsp chopped fresh mint

1 tbsp chopped fresh cilantro

½ tsp ground cumin

½ tsp ground coriander

pinch or two of chili powder

salt and freshly ground black pepper

juice and grated zest of ¼ large orange

juice and grated zest of ½ lime

3 egg whites, lightly beaten

8 tbsp all-purpose flour

2½ cups (600ml) stock (see page 30)

2½ cups (600ml) dry red wine

4–6 red or yellow peppers, cored, seeded, peeled, and cut into strips (see page 34)

finely chopped fresh cilantro, to garnish

1 Mix together thoroughly the pork, eggplant, scallions, 3 tablespoons of bread crumbs, herbs, spices, salt and pepper, and the citrus juices and zest (use your hands for best results). Cook a tiny piece of the mixture in a nonstick skillet and taste for seasoning, adjusting as necessary.

2 Form the mixture into 8–10 oval-shaped sausage patties.

3 Pour the egg whites into a soup plate. Spread the flour on another plate. Sprinkle the remaining bread crumbs on yet another plate and season lightly with salt and pepper.

4 Dredge each sausage patty on all sides in flour, then coat each one in egg white and then in the crumbs. Press firmly to make sure that the crumbs adhere during cooking. Set aside.

5 Mist a heavy nonstick skillet lightly with oil-water spray, and heat. Put in the sausages. Cook over moderately high heat until crusty and browned on one side, then turn carefully and cook on the second side until crusty brown. Transfer the sausages to a warm plate.

6 Pour approximately 1½ cups (350ml) each of the stock and wine into the skillet. Boil rapidly for a few seconds, deglazing the pan by scraping up the browned bits of sausage on the bottom. Add another ¾ cup (175ml) each of stock and wine.

7 Return the sausages to the pan. Simmer over medium heat for several minutes, turning them carefully from time to time.

8 When the sausages are beautifully glazed and the pan juices are reduced, thick, and syrupy, transfer the sausages and sauce to a platter and cover loosely with a tent of foil to keep warm. If you are serving the sausages with a sauce or salsa, as I suggest above, the platter could have a layer of warmed sauce on it, with the sausages arranged on top.

9 Meanwhile, pour the remaining stock and wine into a second skillet or a wok and add the pepper strips. Stir-fry until the peppers are tender and the pan juices are rich and syrupy. Serve the sausages with the pepper strips and garnish the dish with the chopped cilantro.

 Per serving

Total fat (g)	6
Saturated fat (g)	2
Unsaturated fat (g)	4
Cholesterol (mg)	38
Sodium (mg)	989
Calories	670

Makes
4 servings

CRUSTY BROILED PORK CUTLETS

These cutlets are splendid served with a colorful vegetable puree sauce and pan-fried mushrooms or Sicilian Vegetable Salsa (see page 63). They also make a magnificent sandwich filling: try them sandwiched between homemade bread with a good salsa, perhaps embellished with stir-fried peppers or Sweet & Sour Red Onions (see page 70). They will make a sandwich to cherish.

INGREDIENTS

salt and freshly ground black pepper

2–3 tbsp all-purpose flour

8 thin boneless pork loin cutlets, ¼–½in (5mm–1cm) thick, total weight ¾lb (400g), trimmed of all fat

4 egg whites, lightly beaten with a few dashes of Tabasco and Worcestershire sauces and ½ tsp balsamic vinegar

about 16 tbsp fresh bread crumbs

a good pinch of paprika

2–3 tbsp grated Parmesan

olive oil-water spray (see page 29)

lemon or lime wedges, to garnish

1 Season the flour and spread it on a plate. Mix together the bread crumbs, paprika, and Parmesan. Dredge the cutlets in the flour, then dip in the egg white mixture, coating each cutlet well. Dredge the cutlets in the crumbs. Re-dip into the egg and then the crumbs. If possible, chill for 1–2 hours to help the coating adhere.

2 Oil-water spray a nonstick baking sheet and heat under a preheated broiler. Remove carefully, respray, and put the cutlets, well spaced, on the sheet. Spray the cutlets. Broil 5in (12cm) from the heat for 3 minutes or so.

3 Turn, spray again, and broil until browned, sizzling, and just cooked through. Serve the cutlets on a warmed platter with lemon or lime wedges and a sauce of your choice (see introduction).

 Per serving

Total fat (g)	12
Saturated fat (g)	5
Unsaturated fat (g)	7
Cholesterol (mg)	80
Sodium (mg)	704
Calories	456

Makes
4 servings

PIQUANT LEMON HERB MEATBALLS

These are delicate, fragrant, and juicy little meatballs. It's the eggplant that imparts the delicacy and juiciness – under ordinary circumstances, meatballs from very lean beef resemble cannonballs. Serve hot or cold, on their own (with lemon and mint), or in pita bread with salsa or relish, or on a bed of sauce, such as Tomato Eggplant Sauce (see page 62).

INGREDIENTS

1lb (500g) extra-lean pork tenderloin, trimmed and ground

3 tbsp lemon juice, plus extra to taste

grated zest of ½ lemon

1 tbsp each chopped fresh cilantro, parsley, and mint

1 tsp each ground cumin and ground coriander

½ tsp ground paprika

several dashes of Tabasco sauce

good pinch of chili powder, or to taste

two small eggplants, roasted, peeled, and chopped (see page 36)

salt and freshly ground black pepper

1 In a large bowl, thoroughly mix together all of the ingredients. Cook a tiny piece of the mixture in a nonstick pan. Taste and add as much salt, pepper, chili powder, or lemon juice as you want for a good, spicy flavor.

2 Form the mixture into small meatballs and place on a platter. Spritz a nonstick skillet with oil-water spray and heat. Pan-fry the meatballs in batches (they should be well spaced) for 4–6 minutes, turning them until they are well browned and just cooked through.

 Per serving

Total fat (g)	6
Saturated fat (g)	3
Unsaturated fat (g)	3
Cholesterol (mg)	47
Sodium (mg)	461
Calories	287

Makes
6 servings

BEEF BRAISED IN RED WINE WITH A RICH GRAVY

Brisket is a remarkable cut of meat. Once the layers of fat have been trimmed away, it is a flattish, lean cut with a deep, satisfying, old-fashioned beefiness. It is by far the best cut for slow cooking. Here it is braised with red wine and vegetables, which are then pureed with the pan juices to form a rich, thick sauce that rivals any traditional gravy. I like plenty of watercress or a dark green salad served alongside.

INGREDIENTS

1 boneless beef brisket, about 4lb (2kg), unrolled and trimmed of all fat

¾ cup (175ml) stock (see page 30), plus extra (see method)

3 large red onions, sliced

3 red peppers, cored, seeded, and cut into strips

1 cup (250ml) dry red wine

¾ cup (175ml) tomato passata

1 large carrot, sliced

8–10 garlic cloves, peeled

1 chili, coarsely chopped (optional)

salt and freshly ground black pepper

1 Oil-water spray a large nonstick skillet. Heat the pan, add the beef, and sear on both sides. Transfer to a plate and loosely cover with foil. Pour out any fat drippings.

2 Blot the pan lightly with paper towels, then pour in the stock and add the onions. Cover and boil for 4–5 minutes. Uncover, reduce the heat, and cook gently.

3 When the onions are brown and almost tender, add the peppers. Stir and cook until the liquid has evaporated and the peppers are tender, adding more stock as needed. Scrape up the browned bits in the pan as you stir.

4 Meanwhile, pour the wine and tomatoes into a pan. Boil until reduced slightly and thickened.

5 Spread the onions and peppers out in a baking dish. Add the carrot, garlic, and chili. Pour in any pan drippings from the beef. Put the meat on the vegetables and season. Pour the wine-tomato mixture over and around the meat.

Per serving

Total fat (g)	21
Saturated fat (g)	9
Unsaturated fat (g)	11
Cholesterol (mg)	180
Sodium (mg)	263
Calories	556

 Oven temperature
350°F/180°C, then 250°F/120°C

 Oven cooking time
3–3½ hours

 Makes
6 servings

6 Cover the dish with foil, making sure it does not touch the meat. Cook in a preheated oven for 1 hour. Reduce the oven temperature to the lower setting and cook for an additional 2–2½ hours, or until very tender.

7 Remove the meat to a plate and cover it. Pour the pan juices and vegetables into a measuring cup, adding any drippings that have accumulated under the meat, and cover. When the beef is cool, wrap in plastic wrap. Chill the beef, juices, and vegetables in the refrigerator for up to two days. (Chilling sets the beef, making it easy to carve into slices.)

8 Skim any fat from the chilled vegetables and juices. Puree the vegetables and drippings in a blender, then rub them through a sieve to make a wonderfully smooth sauce.

9 Carve the meat thin against the grain and arrange in a baking dish. Pour over some of the pureed vegetable sauce. Either reheat or cover with plastic wrap and chill until ready to use. To reheat, cover the baking dish with foil and cook for 35–40 minutes in an oven preheated to moderate, 325°F/160°C. Reheat the remaining sauce and serve in a warmed gravy boat.

—— PAN-SAUTEED BEEF STEAK IN RED WINE GARLIC SAUCE ——

It is essential to use good beef for this. Many supermarkets are now carrying excellent quality beef, which is worth the extra expense. I would serve these steaks with Oven-Fried Potatoes (see page 72) and watercress. When the ingredients are top-notch, it makes a great dish.

INGREDIENTS

freshly ground black pepper

2 sirloin steaks, each about 5oz (150g), cut ¼–½in (5mm–1cm) thick, trimmed of fat

salt

1 small red onion, quartered and thinly sliced

2–3 garlic cloves, crushed

several dashes of Tabasco sauce

1¼ cups (300ml) dry red wine

1¼ cups (300ml) stock (see page 30)

1½ tbsp Dijon mustard

1 Grind a generous amount of pepper onto a plate, place the steaks on the pepper, and grind more on top. Press the pepper into the steaks.

2 Spritz a heavy-bottomed nonstick skillet with oil-water spray and heat until it sizzles. Lay the steaks, well spaced, in the pan and season them with salt. Sear the steaks over high heat for about 1 minute, turn, salt lightly, and sear for another minute. Transfer the steaks to a plate.

3 Add the onion, garlic, Tabasco, and ½ cup (125ml) each of wine and stock. Cover and boil rapidly for 2–3 minutes, then uncover and simmer briskly until the onions are tender and the juices have reduced to a syrupy sauce. Add the drippings that have accumulated under the steaks.

4 Put the steaks in the pan and cook in the sauce, turning frequently, for 1–2 minutes, or according to taste. Return to the plate and cover loosely with foil.

5 Add the remaining wine and stock to the pan and boil until reduced by just over half and the alcohol has completely evaporated. Whisk in the mustard and simmer briskly for 2 minutes to thicken the sauce and blend the flavors. Return the steaks to the pan and turn them in the sauce until warmed through. Serve the steaks with the sauce poured over the top.

 Per serving

Total fat (g)	11
Saturated fat (g)	4
Unsaturated fat (g)	6
Cholesterol (mg)	81
Sodium (mg)	556
Calories	282

 Makes
2 servings

VENISON STEAKS WITH GRILLED PEPPER PUREE

Venison is a remarkably low-fat, flavored meat. Even farmed venison has a hint of wild gaminess, certainly more so than beef, and it marries well with assertive, but not overwhelming, flavors. Here, it is served with a smoky broiled pepper puree and an onion preserve flavored with a bitter orange marmalade.

INGREDIENTS

For the onion preserve

2 large red onions, halved and sliced into thin crescents

6 large garlic cloves, crushed

juice of ½ large orange

1 tbsp lemon juice

1½ cups (350ml) stock (see page 30)

¾ cup (175ml) dry red wine

1 tsp Seville orange marmalade

2 tsp Dijon mustard

several dashes of Tabasco sauce

dash or two of Worcestershire sauce

For the pepper puree

2 red or yellow peppers, broiled (see page 35)

salt and freshly ground black pepper

For the venison steaks

black peppercorns

4 venison steaks cut 1–1½in (2.5–3.5 cm) thick, each about ¼lb (125g)

1–2 tbsp dry red wine

1–2 tbsp stock (see page 30)

1 For the preserve, put the onions, garlic, citrus juices, 1¼ cups (300ml) of stock and ½ cup (125ml) of wine in a heavy-bottomed, nonstick skillet. Cover, bring to a boil, and simmer briskly for 5–7 minutes.

2 Remove the cover and continue to cook rapidly until the liquid is almost gone and the onions are tender but not mushy, and "frying" in their own juices.

3 Stir in the remaining stock and wine and simmer briskly for a few seconds. Stir in the marmalade, mustard, and sauces. Simmer for another 1–2 minutes, until the preserve has thickened and the flavors have blended. Set the preserve aside.

4 To make the pepper puree, puree the peppers in a blender until smooth. Season with salt and pepper and heat gently. Set aside and keep warm.

5 For the venison, grind a generous amount of pepper onto a plate. Press the venison steaks onto the pepper and grind more pepper on top of them.

6 Spritz a heavy-bottomed nonstick pan with oil-water spray and heat until hot and sizzling. Cook the steaks over high heat, turning them two or three times, until well browned on the outside but still quite rare.

7 Pour the wine and stock into the pan. Continue cooking for about 5 minutes, until the venison is glazed and cooked through, but still pinkish inside. The meat should feel springy (not hard or mushy). Remove to a warm plate.

SERVING THE VENISON

1 Pour the preserve into the pan in which the steaks were cooked. Bring to a boil and simmer for a few minutes, scraping up any browned bits on the bottom of the pan, until the preserve is heated through.

2 Pour the warm pepper puree onto a heated serving platter. Slice the venison steaks across the grain and arrange on the puree. Spoon the preserve over the top.

3 A green vegetable, such as baby spinach or ruby chard, or finely sliced zucchini, makes an excellent accompaniment.

Per serving

Total fat (g)	3
Saturated fat (g)	1
Unsaturated fat (g)	2
Cholesterol (mg)	63
Sodium (mg)	237
Calories	220

Makes
4 servings

FISH & SHELLFISH

FISH IS SUPERB FOOD from both a nutritional and a gastronomic point of view. Low in calories, high in protein and B vitamins, it is a dietitian's dream. The fat content of fish varies with the kind, but even fatty fish is believed to be healthy. Recent scientific and medical studies suggest that the Omega-3 fatty acids in fish oils have a beneficial effect on the heart. Overcooked fish is dry and unpalatable, so cook fish just long enough to become opaque. A good rule of thumb for roasting and oven poaching is to measure the fish at its thickest point, and then to cook at high heat for 9–10 minutes per 1in (2.5cm) of thickness.

CAJUN PRAWNS

This dish was inspired by a New Orleans classic that calls for a pound of butter and a loaf of crusty bread to sop it all up. The butter is history (oh, my arteries!) but the bread is a great idea – the juices, even without the fat, are fabulous and just beg to be soaked up.

INGREDIENTS

4 garlic cloves

4 black olives (Calamata, if possible), slivered off their pits

1 red chili, seeded and finely chopped

1 tbsp snipped fresh rosemary

1 tsp paprika

1 tsp green peppercorns in brine, plus 1 tsp of the brine

about 2 tbsp lemon juice

1¼ cups (300ml) chicken or vegetable stock (see page 30)

salt and freshly ground black pepper

2 dashes of Worcestershire sauce

¾ cup (175ml) fish stock (see page 30)

2lb (1kg) king prawns or jumbo shrimp, shelled and deveined

For the garnish

chopped fresh flat-leaf parsley

torn fresh oregano leaves

1 Crush the garlic and olives together into a pulp. Place in a wok with all the ingredients up to and including the Worcestershire sauce. Bring to a boil and reduce by about two thirds.

2 Add the fish stock, bring back to a boil, and reduce the liquid by half again. Put in the prawns and stir over the highest heat for about 3 minutes, until pink and beginning to curl. Take care not to overcook them or they will turn mealy; taste one to check.

3 Sprinkle with the fresh herbs and serve at once with Flavor-Infused Bulgur (see page 114) or a good dish of rice.

VARIATIONS

Cajun Mussels: replace the prawns with 2lb (1kg) cleaned mussels (discarding any that do not close when tapped). Using a deep, heavy-bottomed saucepan instead of the wok, follow step 1, above. Add the fish stock and bring to a boil. Put in the mussels and cook until they open, 4–6 minutes. Shake the pan halfway through cooking and discard any mussels that do not open. Sprinkle with the herbs.

Cajun Monkfish: slice the 2 fillets from a skinned and boned monkfish tail (see page 103) into ½in (1cm) medallions. Follow step 1, above. Add the fish stock and reduce by half. Set aside while cooking the monkfish. Oil-water spray a nonstick heavy-bottomed skillet, add the monkfish, and sear on both sides to seal. Pour in the reduced liquid and bring back to a boil. Sprinkle with the fresh herbs.

Per serving

Total fat (g)	2
Saturated fat (g)	neg
Unsaturated fat (g)	1
Cholesterol (mg)	488
Sodium (mg)	762
Calories	220

Makes
4 servings

CAJUN PRAWNS *with the hot flavor of chilies.*

MUSSELS STEAMED IN HERBED WHITE WINE

I like serving these mussels piled high on a beautiful platter, as a first course on their own, or as part of an antipasto selection. This recipe is also wonderful with fresh small clams.

INGREDIENTS

2lb (1kg) mussels

1¼ cups (300ml) dry white wine or dry white vermouth

⅔ cup (150ml) water

1 large onion, finely chopped

4 scallions, trimmed and sliced

2 tbsp chopped fresh parsley

4 sprigs fresh thyme

1 double quantity eggplant infusion (see page 62: Bolognese Sauce, step 1)

1–2 tbsp bread crumbs

grated Parmesan, to garnish (optional)

1 Scrub the mussels to remove any grit and traces of barnacles, and pull and scrape away their wispy beards. Discard any mussels that are cracked or abnormally heavy. Tap and squeeze any mussels that are not tightly closed. If they do not immediately close tight, discard them. Swish the remaining mussels around in a large bowl of cold water, drain, then rinse and drain once more.

2 Put the wine, water, onion, scallions, and herbs in a deep, heavy pan. Bring to a boil.

3 Put in the mussels and cover the pan. Simmer for 4–6 minutes, until they open. Using oven mitts, pick up the pan half-way through and give it a good shake. Discard any mussels that do not open.

4 Roughly puree the eggplant infusion in a food processor. Stir in the bread crumbs. When the mussels are cooked, preheat the broiler. Remove the top shell from each mussel. Top the mussel meat within its shell with a spoonful of the eggplant mixture. If you like cheese with shellfish, sprinkle with a little grated Parmesan. Put briefly under the broiler to brown, then serve at once.

 Per serving

Total fat (g)	6.5
Saturated fat (g)	1.5
Unsaturated fat (g)	4.5
Cholesterol (mg)	103
Sodium (mg)	1028
Calories	375

 Makes
4 servings

TUNA MARINATED IN LEMON & GARLIC

Tuna is a substantial fish, disastrously dry when overcooked, juicy and meaty when properly cooked. It is at its best when still slightly pink in the center. To achieve perfect results, cook it for a little less time than is usually recommended for cooking fish (see section introduction, page 100).

INGREDIENTS

2 tuna steaks, each ¾–1in (1.5–2.5cm) thick

½–⅔ cup (125–150ml) freshly squeezed lemon juice

2 tbsp dry white vermouth

2 garlic cloves, crushed

freshly ground black pepper

6 tbsp each red and yellow Pepper Sauces (see page 64)

1 Place the tuna in a baking dish. Sprinkle with ½ cup (125ml) of lemon juice. Sprinkle on the vermouth and garlic, and season with pepper. Turn the fish in the marinade a few times. Cover with plastic wrap and chill for a few hours or overnight. Turn once or twice during marinating.

2 Bring to room temperature. If most of the marinade has been absorbed into the fish, sprinkle with a tablespoon of lemon juice.

3 Bake the fish, uncovered, in a preheated oven for 8–9 minutes, until a bit rare and not at all dry. Serve at once on a bed of the red and yellow pepper sauces.

VARIATION

Substitute fresh swordfish for tuna. The same rules of rareness apply.

Per serving

Total fat (g)	7
Saturated fat (g)	2
Unsaturated fat (g)	5
Cholesterol (mg)	42
Sodium (mg)	106
Calories	265

 Oven temperature
450°F/230°C

 Cooking time
9 minutes

 Makes
2 servings

ROASTED MONKFISH WITH GARLIC SAUCE

Until quite recently, monkfish was often called "poor man's lobster" because of the delicate flavor of its pearly white flesh. Today, we appreciate monkfish not just for its flavor and lack of bones, but for its firm flesh, ideal for roasting or barbecuing. The ruby dark, winey sauce in this recipe sets the flesh off perfectly.

INGREDIENTS

12 garlic cloves, peeled

1 cup (200ml) dry red wine

1 cup (200ml) stock (see page 30)

oil-water spray (see page 29)

2 x ¼lb (125g) monkfish fillets, skin and membrane removed (see below)

salt and freshly ground black pepper

2 sun-dried tomatoes, chopped

1½ tsp Dijon mustard

chopped fresh flat-leaf parsley, to garnish

1 Put 10 of the garlic cloves in a saucepan with ½ cup (125ml) each of wine and stock. Simmer until the garlic is meltingly tender and coated in syrupy glaze.

2 Reduce the garlic to a puree by pushing it through a fine-meshed sieve into a bowl. Set aside. Roughly crush the 2 remaining garlic cloves and set aside.

3 Oil-spray an ovenproof skillet and heat it on the stove. When smoking, quickly brown the monkfish on all sides, turning it, for a total of 1½–2 minutes. Season with salt and pepper.

4 Put the skillet into a preheated oven and bake for 7 minutes. Do not overcook the fish, which should be juicy and pearly (not tough, dry, and fibrous). When pressed with a finger, the fillets should feel firm yet springy.

5 Meanwhile, put the crushed garlic in a saucepan with the remaining stock and wine, and sun-dried tomatoes. Boil for 2–3 minutes, until reduced by half, then whisk in the mustard and the pureed garlic mixture and simmer gently for another minute.

6 Transfer the monkfish to a carving board and slice into ½in (1cm) medallions. Overlap them on a warm plate and spoon the garlic sauce around the slices. Sprinkle with parsley and serve at once. Yellow vegetables, such as yellow tomato slices or yellow pepper strips, make vivid accompaniments for this dish.

Per serving	
Total fat (g)	2
Saturated fat (g)	neg
Unsaturated fat (g)	1
Cholesterol (mg)	18
Sodium (mg)	196
Calories	156

Oven temperature
425°F/220°C

Oven cooking time
7 minutes

Makes
2 servings

PREPARING MONKFISH

1 Using kitchen scissors or a very sharp small knife, and cutting close to the flesh, snip off the two fins from the monkfish and discard them.

2 Pull off and discard the skin and tough membrane covering the monkfish, being careful not to tear the flesh.

3 Using a large chef's knife or a fish filleting knife, slice down one side of the backbone, keeping as close to the bone as possible, to remove the first fillet in one piece.

4 Cut along the other side of the backbone to remove the second fillet, again in one piece. (Do not discard the backbone, which may be used to make a fish stock.)

SALMON WITH YELLOW PEPPER & TARRAGON SAUCE

Salmon is a fatty fish, but the Omega-3 fatty acids in fish oil are believed to be very heart-healthy. This Technicolor extravaganza (coral-tinted fish, blazing yellow sauce, pastel salsa) complements the moist, delicate fish very well indeed.

INGREDIENTS

2 cups (450ml) yellow Pepper Sauce (see page 64 and step 1 below)

2 salmon fillets, each 5–6oz (150–180g)

freshly ground mixed peppercorns

salt

oil-water spray (see page 29)

2 sprigs fresh tarragon

1 quantity Mango & Fennel Salsa (see page 61)

1 Prepare the yellow Pepper Sauce according to the recipe on page 64, but replace the garlic and chili with a pinch of cayenne and a teaspoon of crumbled dried tarragon.

2 Season the salmon on both sides with a generous amount of ground mixed pepper and salt. Spray a skillet with oil-water spray and heat on the stove. Sear the salmon on both sides, flesh side first, for 1½ minutes total, until browned.

3 Immediately cover the pan tightly, remove from the heat, and leave for 3–4 minutes, until the salmon is just done. The flesh should remain sweetly moist and succulent.

4 Coat two plates with a layer of sauce and center a fillet on each one. Top with a sprig of fresh tarragon and surround with Mango & Fennel Salsa.

Per serving

Total fat (g)	20
Saturated fat (g)	3
Unsaturated fat (g)	15
Cholesterol (mg)	83
Sodium (mg)	176
Calories	505

Makes
2 servings

HALIBUT ROASTED IN TOMATO EGGPLANT SAUCE

Halibut is delicious roasted on a bed of velvety Tomato Eggplant Sauce (see page 62). It is important the fish sits on the sauce: don't swamp it by pouring the sauce over the top. Cooked this way, the fillets melt in the mouth.

INGREDIENTS

¾lb (375g) small new potatoes (about 16)

2 halibut fillets, each 6–8oz (180–250g), any bones removed with tweezers

salt and freshly ground black pepper

2½ cups (600ml) Tomato Eggplant Sauce (see page 62)

For the garnish

torn fresh basil leaves

fresh flat-leaf parsley, roughly chopped

1 Bring a pan of water to a boil. Meanwhile, rinse the potatoes under cold running water. When the water is boiling, steam the potatoes in a steamer over the water for 15–20 minutes, until just done.

2 Season the halibut fillets with salt and pepper.

3 Pour the Tomato Eggplant Sauce into an ovenproof skillet, casserole, or baking dish that will hold the fillets in one uncrowded layer. Bring to a boil and let the sauce simmer for a few minutes.

4 Set the fillets, spaced well apart, in the bubbling sauce and arrange the potatoes all around. Immediately transfer the uncovered dish to a preheated oven. Oven-roast the fillets for 9–10 minutes per 1in (2.5cm) thickness of fish (see section introduction, page 100).

5 Scatter the basil and parsley over the top and serve the halibut straight from the pan, onto well-warmed plates.

Per serving

Total fat (g)	6
Saturated fat (g)	1
Unsaturated fat (g)	5
Cholesterol (mg)	90
Sodium (mg)	355
Calories	378

Oven temperature
450°F/230°C

Cooking time
9–10 minutes per 1 inch (2.5cm) thickness of fish

Makes
2 servings

ROASTED BLACK BEAN COD

Marinate the cod with ginger, then roast it quickly in a hot oven so that it falls into ineffably moist, milky flakes. Set off that moist milkiness with a salty, peppery black bean sauce and encircle with a fresh tomato-based salsa.

INGREDIENTS

1 large garlic clove

½in (1cm) piece fresh ginger, peeled

2 tsp teriyaki sauce

1 tsp rice wine vinegar

1 cod fillet, about ¾lb (375g)

freshly ground black pepper

oil-water spray (see page 29)

1 quantity Black Bean Tomato Sauce (see page 66)

1 quantity Chinese Tomato Salsa (see page 67)

1 Crush together the garlic and ginger and put in a bowl with the teriyaki sauce and vinegar.

2 Put the cod on a plate and cover with the garlic-ginger mixture. Grind over some pepper. Marinate at room temperature for approximately 20 minutes.

3 Mist a baking sheet with oil-water spray. Put the cod on the sheet, scraping all the marinade over the fish. Spray with oil-water and oven-roast for 9–10 minutes per 1in (2.5cm) thickness of fish.

4 Spoon the heated Black Bean Tomato Sauce onto a plate, set the roasted fish on top, then surround with the Chinese Tomato Salsa.

Per serving	
Total fat (g)	4
Saturated fat (g)	1
Unsaturated fat (g)	3
Cholesterol (mg)	86
Sodium (mg)	1571
Calories	304

 Oven temperature
425°F/220°C

 Baking time
9–10 minutes per 1 inch (2.5cm) thickness of fish

 Makes
2 servings

PASTA

PASTA IS EXEMPLARY FOOD: quick to cook, inspiring in its variety, supremely comforting, and very low in fat. Traditional pasta sauces, however, are very high fat, laden as they are with butter, olive oil, and fatty cheeses. But it doesn't have to be that way. Sauces based on vegetables, vegetable stock, low- and medium-fat cheeses, with lively seasonings and plenty of fresh herbs, make luscious pasta dressings and are nutritionally savvy. I like sauces to be plentiful, so I ladle them over the pasta with abandon. A serving of pasta is anything from 2–5oz (60–150g), depending on how it is to be served and the sauce accompanying it.

PASTA WITH AN ASIAN AIR

Dress a tangle of the thinnest pasta with an Asian sauce studded with mushrooms, zucchini, and salty black beans, and top the whole thing with Chinese Tomato Salsa for an exuberant vegetarian dish. If you crave meat, add a few slices of pork tenderloin roasted in Korean Pork Marinade (see page 93).

INGREDIENTS

½in (1cm) piece of fresh ginger, peeled

2 garlic cloves

1 red onion, cut into chunks

1¼ cups (300ml) chicken or vegetable stock (see page 30)

¼lb (125g) mushrooms, quartered

¼ cup (60ml) sherry

dash or two of teriyaki sauce

¾lb (375g) zucchini, trimmed and diced

½lb (250g) vermicelli (preferably angel hair)

½ cup (125ml) passata

2 tbsp black bean sauce

2 tbsp hoisin sauce

2 tbsp Chinese chili sauce

a few drops of lime juice

For the garnish

chopped fresh cilantro

2 or 3 scallions, including the green tops, sliced

1 quantity Chinese Tomato Salsa (see page 67)

1 Crush together the ginger and garlic and put in a wok with the onion and stock. Simmer briskly until reduced by half.

2 Add the mushrooms, sherry, and teriyaki sauce. Simmer briskly for a few minutes, stirring constantly, until the mushrooms are slightly more than half-cooked. Add the zucchini, stir, and cook for 2–3 minutes, until tender but still crisp.

3 Meanwhile, bring a pot of lightly salted water to a boil and cook the vermicelli until tender, about 3 minutes. Drain, cover, and keep warm.

4 Whisk together the passata, black bean sauce, hoisin and Chinese chili sauces, and stir into the wok. Simmer for 2 minutes, until bubbling and thickened, then squeeze in a few drops of lime juice to taste.

5 Toss the sauce with the warm vermicelli. Top each serving with cilantro, scallions, and a generous spoonful of the Chinese Tomato Salsa.

Per serving

Total fat (g)	3
Saturated fat (g)	1
Unsaturated fat (g)	2
Cholesterol (mg)	0
Sodium (mg)	979
Calories	317

Makes
4 servings

PASTA WITH AN ASIAN AIR *combines several Chinese flavorings for an exotic and unusual pasta sauce.*

OPEN RAVIOLI WITH TWO SAUCES

This memorable first course is easy to put together if you have everything ready. Cook the asparagus and sauces ahead of time: briefly steam the asparagus (they should be hot, not overcooked) and have the sauces simmering on the stove before serving.

INGREDIENTS

4 fresh lasagna sheets

1¼ cups (300ml) yellow Pepper Sauce (see page 64)

8 asparagus stalks, cooked (see page 78)

1¼ cups (300ml) Tomato Sauce (see page 66)

freshly ground mixed pepper

1 Cook the lasagna according to package directions, or until tender. Drain and blot. Put one sheet on each of two warm plates.

2 Spoon some Pepper Sauce on the pasta, and top each one with four asparagus spears. Cover with a lasagna sheet, placing it at an angle. Pour on the Tomato Sauce, and season. Serve at once.

Per serving

Total fat (g)	4
Saturated fat (g)	1
Unsaturated fat (g)	2
Cholesterol (mg)	0
Sodium (mg)	272
Calories	358

Makes
2 servings

FARFALLE WITH MINTED PEA PUREE

A subtly flavored, brilliant green pea puree, redolent of mint and lime, makes a highly successful sauce for this pasta shape. Toss peas, crisp asparagus tips, and pieces of vivid peppers on top for an exhilarating contrast of colors and textures.

INGREDIENTS

¼lb (125g) petits pois

¼lb (125g) asparagus tips

3 peppers (1 red, 1 yellow, and 1 orange), peeled and seeded (see page 35)

1¼ cups (300ml) stock (see page 30)

¾lb (375g) farfalle

1 quantity pea puree (see Variation, page 50), thinned with a little stock

1 tbsp lime juice

torn fresh mint leaves, to garnish

1 Steam the petit pois and asparagus tips until just done but still bright green. Cut the peppers into 1in (2.5cm) squares and sauté in the stock, as in the recipe for Silky Stir-Fried Sweet Pepper Strips (see page 71).

2 Cook the farfalle according to package instructions, until *al dente*. Warm the pea puree and stir in the lime juice, then toss with the farfalle and vegetables. Scatter the mint and serve at once.

Per serving

Total fat (g)	4
Saturated fat (g)	1
Unsaturated fat (g)	3
Cholesterol (mg)	0
Sodium (mg)	162
Calories	462

Makes
4 servings

MUSHROOM-INFUSED PASTA

A simple recipe that infuses pasta shells with the essence of wild mushrooms. This is a wonderful companion for mushroom ragouts, pork tenderloin, and roasted chicken.

INGREDIENTS

1½ cups (350ml) vegetable or chicken stock (see page 30)

1¼ cups (300ml) mushroom-soaking stock (see page 30)

3 scallions, trimmed and thinly sliced

salt and freshly ground black pepper

pinch of chili powder

dash or two of Tabasco sauce

½lb (250g) tiny pasta shells

3 tbsp each chopped fresh flat-leaf parsley and snipped fresh chives

1 Put the liquids and scallions in a heavy-bottomed pan. Season with salt, pepper, chili powder, and Tabasco. Bring to a boil.

2 Add the pasta, stir, and bring to a boil. Cover tightly, reduce to the lowest heat, and leave for 7 minutes, or until *al dente*. Uncover and stir. Remove from the heat, drape a dish towel over the pan, cover, and leave for 5 minutes. The pasta should be tender and most of the liquid absorbed. Stir in the herbs and serve.

Per serving

Total fat (g)	1
Saturated fat (g)	<1
Unsaturated fat (g)	<1
Cholesterol (mg)	0
Sodium (mg)	92
Calories	238

Makes
4 servings, as an accompaniment

LINGUINE WITH MUSHROOM CREAM SAUCE

Who would guess that the wickedly creamy sauce here is made with skim milk, skim milk powder, and cornstarch? It sounds appallingly austere, but in reality it is rich and indulgent. The dried porcini pieces and the sherry are the secret ingredients – they make the sauce memorable.

INGREDIENTS

4 garlic cloves, crushed

1 tbsp each snipped fresh rosemary and thyme leaves

4 black olives, slivered off their pits

4 sun-dried tomatoes, chopped

2½ cups (600ml) stock (see page 30)

1½lb (750g) mushrooms

½oz (15g) dried porcini, rinsed and finely snipped (see page 30)

¼ cup (60ml) dry sherry

1 tbsp teriyaki sauce

several dashes of Tabasco sauce

3 tbsp skim milk powder

2 tbsp cornstarch

1¼ cups (400ml) skim milk, plus extra (see method)

1lb (500g) dried linguine

3 tbsp freshly grated Parmesan

1½ tbsp spicy mustard

1 tbsp snipped fresh oregano leaves

salt and freshly ground black pepper

1 Put the garlic, rosemary, thyme, olives, sun-dried tomatoes, and 1¼ cups (300ml) of stock into a wok. Boil until the liquid is almost entirely evaporated.

2 Add the mushrooms, dried porcini, sherry, and sauces. Pour in ⅔ cup (150ml) of stock and cook over high heat, stirring, for about 3 minutes, until the liquid has evaporated. Pour in the remaining stock. Cook for 5–7 minutes, stirring, until the mushrooms are just tender and have released their liquid.

3 Meanwhile, mix the milk powder and cornstarch in a measuring cup. Whisk in the skim milk rapidly to avoid lumps forming. Slowly stir this mixture into the sauce and cook for a minute or so until thick and bubbling. Bring a pot of lightly salted water to a boil. Add the linguine and cook until *al dente*.

4 Meanwhile, add the Parmesan, mustard, and oregano to the sauce. Cook, stirring, for 3 minutes. If needed, stir in a little more milk to make a silky sauce. Taste, and season. Drain the pasta and toss with the hot sauce.

Per serving

Total fat (g)	9
Saturated fat (g)	4
Unsaturated fat (g)	5
Cholesterol (mg)	14
Sodium (mg)	835
Calories	655

Makes
4 servings

CONCHIGLIE WITH CHUNKY PEPPERS & HERBS

An extravagance of colorful peppers sautéed in stock to the point of silky tenderness, then tossed with basil, parsley, and pasta shells or quills makes a good dish for an informal meal.

INGREDIENTS

10 mixed red or yellow peppers, peeled, seeded, and cut into 1in (2.5cm) squares (see page 34)

2 fresh chilies, seeded and finely chopped

4 garlic cloves, coarsely chopped

1½ cups (350ml) stock (see page 30)

1lb (500g) conchiglie, penne, or other short pasta shape

15 fresh basil leaves, shredded

1 tbsp chopped fresh parsley

1 Mix together the pepper squares, chilies, garlic, and stock in a heavy-bottomed skillet, and cook, stirring occasionally, until the peppers are tender and bathed in a syrupy sauce.

2 Cook the pasta according to package instructions until *al dente*, then drain and combine with the sauce.

3 Toss in the basil leaves and parsley and serve at once.

Per serving

Total fat (g)	4
Saturated fat (g)	1
Unsaturated fat (g)	3
Cholesterol (mg)	0
Sodium (mg)	108
Calories	573

Makes
4 servings

GRILLED VEGETABLE LASAGNA

This is a simple, colorful lasagna of grilled vegetables, vivid sauce, and herbs. Oven-ready lasagna sheets are better if you blanch them for 3 minutes before putting the lasagna together. The dish will then need less cooking. If desired, top the lasagna with Ricotta Parmesan Custard (see page 80) and a sprinkling of Parmesan or mozzarella before baking it (as illustrated below).

INGREDIENTS

½lb (250g) oven-ready lasagna sheets (about 9 sheets)

salt

3¼ cups (900ml) Tomato, Garlic & Pepper Sauce (see page 64)

2 eggplants, sliced and broiled (see basic recipe, page 81)

4 zucchini, sliced and broiled (see basic recipe, page 81)

about 3 tbsp each chopped fresh flat-leaf parsley and torn basil leaves

1 Blanch the lasagna sheets in rapidly boiling salted water for 3 minutes, stirring to keep the sheets separate. Refresh by running cold water into the pan until cool, then lift out and place in one layer on dish towels.

2 Spread a spoonful of the sauce in a baking dish. Top with 3 lasagna sheets. Spread some sauce over. Cut the vegetables into ¾in (1.5cm) pieces and scatter with some herbs over the sauce. Cover with 3 sheets of lasagna. Spread on more sauce and scatter the remaining vegetables and herbs. Top with 3 lasagna sheets and cover with the remaining sauce.

3 Cover the dish with foil, shiny side in. The dish should be well sealed, but the foil should not touch the top of the lasagna.

4 Bake in a preheated oven for 15 minutes, then uncover and bake for 15–20 minutes, until the lasagna is hot throughout.

5 Remove the lasagna from the oven and let sit for 5 minutes before cutting into squares to serve. Sprinkle some chopped herbs over each serving.

 Per serving

Total fat (g)	2
Saturated fat (g)	<1
Unsaturated fat (g)	1
Cholesterol (mg)	0
Sodium (mg)	97
Calories	215

 Oven temperature
350°F/180°C

 Baking time
30–35 minutes

 Makes
6 servings

CONCHIGLIONI WITH CREAMY BROCCOLI PESTO

What a wonderful way to eat your broccoli: folded into Quark and ricotta with basil, Parmesan, and a few slivers of olives, then put into large pasta shells and baked under a mantle of chunky Tomato Sauce.

INGREDIENTS

18 giant pasta shells (conchiglioni)

3½oz (100g) Quark (if unavailable, use all ricotta, 8oz (240g) in total recipe)

4½oz (140g) ricotta

6oz (180g) steamed broccoli, roughly chopped

2oz (60g) fresh flat-leaf parsley, roughly chopped

handful of fresh basil (about 12 leaves), torn

3 black olives, slivered off their pits

4 tbsp grated Parmesan

2oz (60g) Italian-style low-fat mozzarella cheese, drained and grated

salt and freshly ground black pepper

dash or two of Tabasco sauce

1 quantity Tomato Sauce (see page 66)

1 Cook the pasta shells according to the package directions, but undercook them slightly. Drain the pasta very well.

2 Put the Quark, ricotta, broccoli, herbs, olives, 3 tablespoons of the Parmesan, and half the mozzarella in a food processor. Season with salt, pepper, and Tabasco. Process to a green-flecked cream.

3 Spoon a layer of the Tomato Sauce onto the bottom of a baking dish large enough to hold all 18 pasta shells.

4 Spoon enough of the broccoli cream into each shell to fill it. Place in the baking dish on the Tomato Sauce. When all the shells are filled and in the dish, spoon more Tomato Sauce over them. Sprinkle with the remaining Parmesan and mozzarella cheeses.

5 Cover the dish with foil so that it is well sealed, but the foil is not touching the contents. Bake in a preheated oven for 15 minutes. Uncover and bake for 15–20 minutes, until the dish is bubbling and the cheese has melted on top.

 Per serving

Total fat (g)	9
Saturated fat (g)	5
Unsaturated fat (g)	4
Cholesterol (mg)	25
Sodium (mg)	394
Calories	356

 Oven temperature
350°F/180°C

 Baking time
30–35 minutes

Makes
6 servings

LASAGNA

Layers of pasta, Bolognese Sauce, and Ricotta Parmesan Custard make a homey, comforting lasagna, perfect for family feasting.

INGREDIENTS

¼ tsp freshly grated nutmeg

1 quantity Ricotta Parmesan Custard (see page 80), uncooked

7oz (200g) oven-ready lasagna sheets

1 quantity Bolognese Sauce (see page 62)

3–4 tbsp freshly grated Parmesan

1 Beat the nutmeg into the Ricotta Parmesan Custard. Parboil, drain, and blot the lasagna sheets, as for Grilled Vegetable Lasagna (see page 110).

2 Spread a generous spoonful of Bolognese Sauce in a baking dish. Top with a layer of lasagna sheets. Spread with more sauce. Pour on a third of the custard. Top with lasagna sheets, more sauce, and half the remaining custard. Finally, top with the remaining lasagna sheets, sauce, and custard. Sprinkle with the Parmesan.

3 Bake, uncovered, for 30–40 minutes in a preheated oven until the custard is set and the top is browned. To check that the custard is set, insert a thin knife into the center of the lasagna.

 Per serving

Total fat (g)	12
Saturated fat (g)	7
Unsaturated fat (g)	5
Cholesterol (mg)	69
Sodium (mg)	385
Calories	346

 Oven temperature
350°F/180°C

 Baking time
30–40 minutes

 Makes
8 servings

GRAINS & LEGUMES

GRAINS AND LEGUMES HAVE NOURISHED POPULATIONS since ancient times. Few foods are as comforting and sustaining. Of course, in too earnest hands they can also be very worthy, stodgy, and dull. But you will not find that sort of '70s health food ethic here. These recipes glow with warmth and comfort and are never leaden. From the vegetable-laced squares of grilled polenta below, alive with the colors and flavors of an imaginative flavor infusion, to the splendid bean stews and lentil and rice dishes later in the section, these dishes are sure to be received with acclaim.

FLAVOR-INFUSED GRILLED POLENTA

I adore polenta, and this is the best I've ever had. It's an extravaganza of color and has an unforgettable flavor because of the flavor infusion – red onions, garlic, wine, sun-dried tomatoes, and olives, with scallions and herbs – into which the polenta is stirred.

INGREDIENTS

7½ cups (1.8 liters) stock (see page 30)

½ cup (125ml) dry red wine

2 red onions, chopped

2 garlic cloves, crushed

4 sun-dried tomatoes, chopped

4 black olives, slivered off their pits

1 chili, seeded and finely chopped

6 scallions, trimmed, cut in half lengthwise, then sliced across finely

salt and freshly ground black pepper

12oz (375g) quick-cooking polenta

2–3 tbsp chopped fresh parsley

oil-water spray (see page 29)

1 Put 1¼ cups (300ml) of the stock and all the wine in a deep, heavy-bottomed saucepan and add the onions, garlic, sun-dried tomatoes, olives, and chili. Cover, bring to a boil, and simmer briskly for 5–7 minutes. Uncover and continue to simmer until the onions are tender and the liquid has greatly reduced.

2 Stir in the scallions and continue to simmer briskly until the liquid is almost gone.

3 Add the remaining stock, season with salt and pepper, and bring to just below a boil.

4 Wearing an oven mitt on your stirring hand because the mixture will bubble furiously, pour in the polenta in a steady stream, whisking with a wire whisk as you do so. When it gets thick, change to a long-handled wooden spoon. Cook for about 5 minutes, still stirring, until smooth and cooked. Stir in the parsley, and taste for seasoning. It should be lively: bland polenta is dire.

5 Spread the polenta on a baking sheet. There may be a small bowlful left over. Save it for a separate meal, unless you want to eat it on the spot. Cover the polenta well and chill in the refrigerator until required.

SERVING THE POLENTA

1 Cut the polenta into squares about 3 x 3in (7 x 7cm). Spray lightly with oil-water spray and broil until lightly browned.

2 Serve the polenta squares hot with a selection of vegetable toppings. Particularly good are Mushrooms Made Wild (see page 74), Glazed Fennel, and Sweet & Sour Red Onions (see page 70), all of which are illustrated here, and Silky Stir-Fried Sweet Pepper Strips (see page 71) and Bolognese Sauce (see page 62).

Per serving

Total fat (g)	3
Saturated fat (g)	1
Unsaturated fat (g)	2
Cholesterol (mg)	0
Sodium (mg)	241
Calories	227

Makes
8 servings

GLAZED FENNEL
(BELOW)

MUSHROOMS
MADE WILD
(RIGHT)

SWEET & SOUR
RED ONIONS
(RIGHT)

FLAVOR-INFUSED BULGUR

A wonderful alternative to rice, bulgur has a nutty taste and tender texture, and soaks up flavor like nobody's business. Red wine gives this dish a mauve/burgundy tint.

INGREDIENTS

2½ cups (600ml) stock (see page 30)

1 red onion, chopped

2 garlic cloves, crushed

4 sun-dried tomatoes, chopped

½–1 chili, seeded and finely chopped

4 black olives, slivered off their pits

salt and freshly ground black pepper

1 cup (180g) bulgur

1 tbsp lemon juice, or to taste

For the garnish

vine-ripened tomatoes or cherry tomatoes, halved or quartered

chopped fresh flat-leaf parsley

1 Put 1 cup (250ml) of the stock, the onion, garlic, sun-dried tomatoes, chili, and olives in a skillet or wok. Bring to a boil, then cover and simmer briskly for 5 minutes. Uncover, and continue to simmer until the onion is tender and cooking in its own juices.

2 Add the remaining stock and bring to a boil. Season with salt and pepper.

3 Put the bulgur in a heatproof bowl and pour in the boiling mixture. Cover and leave for 30 minutes, until the bulgur is tender and the liquid absorbed.

4 Uncover and squeeze in lemon juice to taste. Taste and add more salt and pepper, if necessary. Drape a dish towel over the bowl and leave for 5 minutes.

5 To serve, mound on a platter, surround with the tomatoes, and sprinkle with parsley. Cajun Prawns (see page 100) go well with this, as do braised chicken, duck, venison, or roast pork.

Per serving

Total fat (g)	2
Saturated fat (g)	1
Unsaturated fat (g)	1
Cholesterol (mg)	0
Sodium (mg)	211
Calories	210

Makes
4 servings

SPICY LIMA BEANS

A generous helping of zesty beans makes a marvelous meal in a bowl with crusty bread, or wrapped in a tortilla with pea puree (see page 50) and a selection of salsas. The variation makes a no-fat "refried" bean-style dip.

INGREDIENTS

2 red onions, chopped

4 garlic cloves, crushed

3 sun-dried tomatoes, chopped

1 chili, seeded and chopped

1 tbsp ground cumin

½ tbsp ground coriander

1¼ cups (375ml) stock (see page 30)

1lb 15oz (950g) can lima beans, drained and rinsed

1¼ cups (300ml) passata

juice of 1 lime, plus extra to taste

2 tbsp each chopped fresh parsley, mint, and cilantro

salt and freshly ground black pepper

1 Put the onions, garlic, sun-dried tomatoes, chili, spices, and 1¼ cups (300ml) of stock in a skillet. Cover and boil for 5–7 minutes. Uncover and simmer briskly until the onions are tender and the liquid is almost gone.

2 Stir in the remaining stock, the beans, and passata. Simmer, partially covered, for 10 minutes, or until thick. Stir in the lime juice and herbs. Taste, and season with salt and pepper.

VARIATION

Bean dip: cool the mixture. Process to a smooth puree, adding extra lime juice. Work in more stock if needed for a soft, creamy texture.

Per serving

Total fat (g)	2
Saturated fat (g)	1
Unsaturated fat (g)	1
Cholesterol (mg)	0
Sodium (mg)	1099
Calories	133

Makes
4 servings

ORANGE-THYME SCENTED WILD RICE

Try serving this wild rice dish with duck and game dishes. The dried berry fruits and the orange juice complement the richer flavors of the meats wonderfully well.

INGREDIENTS

1 large red onion, chopped

pinch of crushed red pepper flakes

3½ cups (825ml) stock (see page 30)

juice of ½ orange

2 tbsp dried sour cherries

2 tbsp dried cranberries

1½ cups (250g) wild rice

2 tsp fresh thyme leaves

salt and freshly ground black pepper

1 Put the chopped onion, the red pepper flakes, 1¼ cups (300ml) of the stock, and the orange juice in a flameproof casserole. Simmer until the onion is tender and the liquid is almost gone. Add the dried cherries and cranberries, rice, and thyme. Stir until well mixed.

2 Pour in the remaining stock and season with salt and pepper. Bring to a boil and cover the casserole tightly.

3 Bake in a preheated oven for 45–55 minutes, until the rice is tender (some of the grains will puff open) and the liquid has been absorbed.

4 Drape a dish towel over the casserole, replace the lid over the towel, and leave for a few minutes. Fluff the rice with a fork before serving.

Per serving

Total fat (g)	1
Saturated fat (g)	neg
Unsaturated fat (g)	1
Cholesterol (mg)	0
Sodium (mg)	189
Calories	314

Oven temperature
350°F/180°C

Baking time
45–55 minutes

Makes
4 servings

BABY LENTILS WITH WILD MUSHROOMS & HERBS

I like Puy lentils for their color, a gorgeous deep green, flecked with turquoise, and their flavor. Both are the result of being grown in volcanic soil around Le Puy in France. Being small lentils, they do not need soaking before use.

INGREDIENTS

3 cups (750ml) mushroom-soaking liquid (see page 30)

3 cups (750ml) stock (see page 30), plus extra (see method)

½ cup (125ml) red wine

2 red onions, chopped

3 garlic cloves, crushed

1½ cups (275g) baby lentils, rinsed and picked over

½oz (15g) porcini mushrooms, soaked and finely chopped (see page 30)

salt and freshly ground black pepper

dash of Tabasco sauce, optional

2 tbsp each chopped fresh oregano and parsley

2 tsp fresh thyme leaves

juice of ½ lemon

1 Put ⅔ cup (150ml) of the mushroom-soaking liquid, ⅔ cup (150ml) of the stock, and all the red wine in a saucepan with the onions and garlic and bring to a boil. Cover and simmer briskly for 5 minutes.

2 Remove the cover and continue to simmer until the onions are tender and cooking in their syrupy juices.

3 Stir in the lentils, porcini, and the remaining mushroom-soaking liquid and stock. Season generously with pepper, bring to a boil, and continue to cook, uncovered, for 10 minutes.

4 Reduce the heat and simmer, partially covered, for 30–35 minutes, stirring occasionally, until the lentils are tender. Add a little more stock if needed to prevent scorching.

5 Season well with salt, and add Tabasco sauce for an extra bite, if you like. Stir in the fresh herbs and the lemon juice.

Per serving

Total fat (g)	2
Saturated fat (g)	neg
Unsaturated fat (g)	2
Cholesterol (mg)	0
Sodium (mg)	188
Calories	281

Makes
4 servings

LIMA BEAN & PROSCIUTTO STEW

I would describe these as sort of heavenly baked beans (they really are marvelous). They are perfectly delicious served ladled onto slices of toasted Wild Mushroom Bread (see page 146), as illustrated below.

INGREDIENTS

olive oil-water spray (see page 29)

3oz (90g) prosciutto, trimmed of fat and diced

1 red onion, chopped

3 garlic cloves, crushed

pinch of crushed red pepper flakes

4 sun-dried tomatoes, chopped

½ tsp ground paprika

⅔ cup (150ml) dry red wine

1 cup (250ml) stock (see page 30)

1 red pepper, broiled, skinned, and diced (see page 35)

1 cup (250ml) passata

1 tbsp Dijon mustard

1 tsp tomato paste

1 tbsp lemon juice

1lb 15oz (950g) can lima beans, drained and rinsed

salt and freshly ground black pepper

1 Spritz a skillet with the oil-water spray. Scatter the prosciutto pieces and heat. When they start to sizzle, stir-fry for 1 minute. Transfer to a small bowl.

2 Add the onion to the pan with the garlic, red pepper flakes, sun-dried tomatoes, and paprika. Pour in the wine and stock, bring the mixture to a boil, and deglaze by scraping up any browned bits on the bottom of the pan.

3 Cover and simmer briskly for 5 minutes. Uncover and simmer until the liquid has gone and the onion is cooking in its own juices.

4 Meanwhile, put the pepper, passata, mustard, tomato paste, and lemon juice in a blender and process to a puree.

5 Stir the beans into the onion mixture, then add the puree and salt and pepper. Simmer gently, partially covered, for 5–7 minutes, or until thickened.

SERVING THE BEANS

Serve the beans on slices of Wild Mushroom Bread (see page 146). Alternatively, heap them onto broiled polenta squares (see page 112) or spicy Sweet Potato Pancakes (see page 73).

Per serving

Total fat (g)	8
Saturated fat (g)	4
Unsaturated fat (g)	4
Cholesterol (mg)	0
Sodium (mg)	1775
Calories	202

Makes
4 servings

RAGOUT OF ROOT VEGETABLES & CANNELLINI BEANS

Root vegetables are in vogue now – I'm glad that chefs are beginning to notice that non-Mediterranean cuisines have something to offer the gastronomic world. The delicious flavors of root vegetables are enhanced by the other ingredients in this dish. The garlic becomes quite gentle and mellow cooked this way.

INGREDIENTS

For the ragout

1 head garlic

1 Spanish onion, halved, then cut into ½in (1cm) wedges

1 fennel bulb, trimmed and cut into ½in (1cm) wedges

1 small rutabaga, peeled and cut into ½in (1cm) pieces

1 large parsnip, peeled and cut into ½in (1cm) pieces

2 carrots, scrubbed and cut into ½in (1cm) slices

2 celery stalks, trimmed and cut into ½in (1cm) pieces

5 cups (1.25 liters) stock (see page 30)

½ tsp dried tarragon, crumbled

1 tbsp Dijon mustard

2 tbsp tomato paste

3–4 dashes of soy sauce

½ cup (125ml) dry red wine

3 tbsp lemon juice

salt and freshly ground black pepper

14oz (425g) can cannellini beans, drained and rinsed

For the garnish

1 quantity White Bean, Orange & Tarragon Puree (see page 67)

fresh tarragon, snipped

1 Separate the head of garlic into individual cloves. Using a wooden mallet, hit them to loosen the skin (see page 35). Remove the skins, but leave the cloves whole.

2 Put the garlic in a large pan with the other vegetables and ½ cup (125ml) of the stock. Cover, bring to a boil, and simmer for approximately 5 minutes. Remove the cover and simmer for another 5 minutes, stirring occasionally.

3 Pour in the remaining stock. Stir all the remaining ingredients except the beans into the ragout and season to taste. Simmer, partially covered, for 40 minutes.

4 Stir in the beans. Taste, and adjust the seasoning, if necessary. Simmer for 10–15 minutes longer, until the ingredients are very tender.

5 Serve in bowls, garnishing each helping with a dollop of the White Bean, Orange & Tarragon Puree and a sprinkling of fresh tarragon.

VARIATION

For a dish with a quite different but equally delicious flavor, replace the rutabaga and parsnip with pumpkin and acorn squash. Replace the tarragon with fresh sage leaves, snipped.

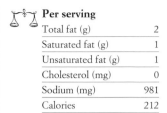

Per serving

Total fat (g)	2
Saturated fat (g)	1
Unsaturated fat (g)	1
Cholesterol (mg)	0
Sodium (mg)	981
Calories	212

Makes
6 servings

CHOCOLATE DESSERTS

LIFE WITHOUT CHOCOLATE is simply too bleak to contemplate. Fortunately, low-fat cocoa powder is pure, deep chocolate and can be used in all sorts of clever ways to produce real chocolate sensuality. Try the Chocolate Roulade, illustrated in this section, or the deceptively simple Chocolate Sorbet, for instance.

In many cases, I use a small amount of semisweet chocolate to round out the flavor of a chocolate recipe. Always choose chocolate that contains at least 70 percent cocoa solids: the higher the cocoa solids content, the lower the amount of cocoa butter. Avoid chocolate made with vegetable fat.

── CHOCOLATE ROULADE ──

This mouth-watering, unbelievably rich-looking roulade is one of my star turns – no one believes it is low fat. The base is a yolk-free soufflé baked flat. Pull out all the stops when decorating the roulade for a special occasion, as in the photograph. For more everyday meals, I give a simpler serving idea.

INGREDIENTS

For the roulade

⅔ cup (180g) superfine sugar

½ cup (60g) low-fat cocoa powder

9 egg whites, at room temperature

pinch of cream of tartar

1½ tsp vanilla extract

1½ tsp dark rum

sifted confectioners' sugar, for sprinkling

For the filling

1 quantity Chestnut Chocolate Cream (see page 120)

small pieces of grated chocolate (see page 43), to decorate

1 Line a (13 x 11in) (32.5 x 28cm) jelly roll pan or baking sheet with nonstick baking parchment.

2 For the roulade, sift together 7 tablespoons superfine sugar with the cocoa powder. Set aside.

3 Whisk the egg whites and the cream of tartar together until foamy. Continuing to whisk briskly, add the remaining superfine sugar, a little at a time, until the mixture holds stiff peaks.

4 Carefully fold the cocoa mixture into the egg whites. Fold in the vanilla and dark rum.

5 Spread the mixture in the prepared pan. Bake in a preheated oven for 20–30 minutes, or until a toothpick inserted in the middle comes out clean. Cool in the pan on a wire rack.

6 Spread a clean dish towel on the work surface. Cover with a sheet of waxed paper or baking parchment, then sprinkle evenly with confectioners' sugar. When thoroughly cooled, invert the roulade base onto the paper, then peel off the parchment.

7 Spread with the Chestnut Chocolate Cream, reserving 3–4 tablespoons, if desired, for decoration. Starting from a long edge, roll up the roulade base like a jelly roll. Use the dish towel to help you. Cover with plastic wrap and chill until needed.

8 To decorate the roulade, put the reserved filling in a pastry bag fitted with a medium nozzle. Pipe rosettes or a shell pattern along the top. Decorate with a few chocolate pieces and dust with confectioners' sugar, if desired.

VARIATION

Ice the roulade with Chocolate Icing (see page 121) and serve with Raspberry Coulis (see page 124).

 Per serving

Total fat (g)	2
Saturated fat (g)	1
Unsaturated fat (g)	1
Cholesterol (mg)	neg
Sodium (mg)	189
Calories	176

 Oven temperature
180°C/350°F/gas 4

 Baking time
20–30 minutes

 Makes
8 servings

CHOCOLATE ROULADE
a delightful finish for a special occasion.

CHESTNUT CHOCOLATE CREAM

This stand-in for high-fat buttercream makes a delicious filling for the Chocolate Roulade (see pages 118–119 or use it to sandwich Vanilla Meringues (see page 149).

INGREDIENTS

½oz (15g) semisweet chocolate (see page 43)

3 tbsp confectioners' sugar

1 tbsp low-fat cocoa powder (see page 43)

4oz (125g) chestnut puree

½ cup (100g) no-fat or very low-fat fromage frais

1 tsp vanilla extract

1 Melt the chocolate in a heatproof bowl over a pan of boiling water and let cool slightly. Sift together the confectioners' sugar and the cocoa powder.

2 Put all of the remaining ingredients into a food processor or blender, then sprinkle in the cocoa mixture. Add the melted chocolate and process until very well combined.

3 Transfer the mixture to a bowl, then cover with plastic wrap and store in the refrigerator until ready to use.

 Per recipe quantity

Total fat (g)	9
Saturated fat (g)	4
Unsaturated fat (g)	5
Cholesterol (mg)	2
Sodium (mg)	143
Calories	547

 Makes
About 1¼ cups (300ml)

CHOCOLATE & RASPBERRY TORTE

Raspberries and chocolate make a magnificent combination, and this torte makes the most of them. It looks splendid, and the fudgy quality of the chocolate base is compelling. The torte is best eaten on the day after it is made.

INGREDIENTS

1¼ cups (165g) self-rising flour

¾ cup (180g) superfine sugar

¼ cup (30g) low-fat cocoa powder (see page 43)

pinch of salt

¾ cup (180g) very low-fat fromage frais

¼ cup (50ml) skim milk

1 tsp vanilla extract

½ cup (125ml) water

1½ pints (625g) fresh raspberries

2 tbsp sugar

slivered zest of ½ orange and ½ lemon

For the decoration

a few raspberries and leaves

small pieces of grated semisweet chocolate (see page 43)

1 Sift together the flour, sugar, cocoa, and salt into a bowl.

2 In a measuring cup, mix the fromage frais, milk, vanilla, and water and pour over the dry ingredients in the bowl. Gently stir together so that the dry ingredients are thoroughly incorporated.

3 Spread the batter evenly in a 9in (23cm) springform pan. Mix together the raspberries (reserve a few for decoration), sugar, and citrus zest. Pour in one even layer over the batter, leaving a ½in (1cm) border all around.

4 Bake in a preheated oven for 30–35 minutes, then let cool. The raspberry center will be wet, but will firm up as the torte cools. Cover with plastic wrap and chill until needed. Before serving, top with raspberries, raspberry leaves, and a little grated chocolate.

 Per serving

Total fat (g)	1
Saturated fat (g)	<1
Unsaturated fat (g)	<1
Cholesterol (mg)	neg
Sodium (mg)	171
Calories	214

 Oven temperature
350°F/180°C

Baking time
30–35 minutes

 Makes
8 servings

CHOCOLATE CREPES

These are lovely, delicate crepes made with virtually no fat at all, just a spritz of oil-water spray. Fill them with orange segments, strawberries or raspberries, and a ricotta cream (see page 137). Alternatively, fill the crepes with apricot preserves, then top with crushed amaretti.

INGREDIENTS

⅔ cup (90g) all-purpose flour

2 tbsp low-fat cocoa powder (see page 43)

4 tbsp superfine sugar

2oz (60g) skim milk powder

¾ cup (175ml) skim milk

4 egg whites

2 tsp vanilla extract

oil-water spray (see page 29)

1 Sift the flour, cocoa, sugar, and milk powder into a bowl. Blend the milk, egg whites, and vanilla in a blender until smooth. Whisk this liquid into the cocoa mixture and let stand for 30 minutes.

2 Oil-water spray a small skillet and heat it on the stove. When it sizzles, carefully spray the pan again; reduce the heat to medium.

3 Using a ladle that holds about ¼ cup (60ml), spoon one ladleful of batter into the hot pan. Immediately tilt and rotate the pan so that the batter covers the bottom in a thin layer. Cook over high heat for a few seconds until the batter bubbles a little. Have ready a sheet of waxed paper.

4 Flip the crepe over. Cook the other side for a few seconds, until the crepe is just set, slides easily around the pan, and is lightly speckled. Slide the crepe onto the waxed paper. Repeat until all the batter is used.

VARIATION

Citrus-Scented Vanilla Crepes: replace the cocoa powder with an extra ¼ cup (30g) plain flour, and add the grated zest of 1 lemon and 1 orange.

 Per crepe

Total fat (g)	neg
Saturated fat (g)	neg
Unsaturated fat (g)	neg
Cholesterol (mg)	1
Sodium (mg)	62
Calories	63

Makes
About 15 crepes

DARK CHOCOLATE ICING

This wonderfully rich all-purpose icing can be used with other recipes in this book, such as the Mocha variation on the Cassata (see page 143). The recipe makes more than you will need to ice the roulade, so try serving the rest on its own as a splendidly rich and creamy old-fashioned chocolate pudding.

INGREDIENTS

9 tbsp low-fat cocoa powder (see page 43)

3 tbsp cornstarch

5 tbsp skim milk powder

8 tbsp superfine sugar

½oz (15g) semisweet chocolate (see page 43), grated

½ tsp vanilla extract

about 2¼ cups (575ml) skim milk

1 Whisk together all the ingredients. Pour the mixture in batches into a blender and blend until very smooth.

2 Rinse a nonstick saucepan with cold water. Pour out the water, but do not dry the pan (this helps reduce scorching).

3 Pour the mixture into the pan and heat on medium heat, stirring continuously, until it begins to bubble rapidly. Do not scrape the bottom of the pan: if any scorching occurs, then the scorched bits will not be stirred into the mixture.

4 Still stirring, cook the mixture for another minute. Pour into a bowl immediately, cover with plastic wrap, and store in the refrigerator until needed.

VARIATION

Mocha Icing: add 2 tablespoons of superfine sugar, and replace ¾ cup (175ml) of the skim milk with the same quantity of cooled black coffee.

 Per recipe quantity

Total fat (g)	15
Saturated fat (g)	9
Unsaturated fat (g)	6
Cholesterol (mg)	22
Sodium (mg)	1595
Calories	1295

 Makes
5 cups (1.25 liters)

CHOCOLATE CHEESECAKE MOUSSE

Pile this seductive mixture into a goblet, pop in an Almond Cookie like a mini cheesecake crust, and you have a chocolate cheesecake with a difference.

INGREDIENTS

6 tbsp low-fat cocoa powder (see page 43)

½ cup (105g) superfine sugar

6 tbsp skim milk powder

½ cup (125ml) cold water

1 tsp vanilla extract

½oz (15g) semisweet chocolate (see page 43), grated

1lb 2oz (550g) ricotta

7oz (200g) Quark (if unavailable, use all ricotta (1lb 9oz (750g) in total)

1 Sift the cocoa powder, sugar, and milk powder together. Put in a blender with the water and vanilla extract added, and blend until very smooth.

2 Rinse a heavy-bottomed nonstick saucepan with cold water. Pour out the water, but do not dry the saucepan (this helps to reduce scorching). Strain the mixture into the pan and stir in the grated chocolate.

3 Heat on medium heat, stirring constantly, until it begins to bubble rapidly. When stirring, do not scrape the bottom of the saucepan: if any scorching does occur, this will ensure that any scorched bits are not stirred into the pudding. Continue cooking and stirring for 1 minute.

4 Remove from the heat and pour immediately into a bowl. Cover with plastic wrap; chill until needed. The sauce will become very thick and fudgy when cooled.

5 Put the cooled sauce and the ricotta and Quark into a blender and process until very smooth and fluffy. Serve the mousse in goblets, perhaps with two Almond Cookie halves (see page 148) or two Vanilla Meringues (see page 149) jutting out at a jaunty angle.

VARIATION

Drain the completed mousse overnight in a sieve lined with cheesecloth, then swirl it into a meringue case (see page 135). Top with raspberries and a little grated semisweet chocolate.

 Per serving

Total fat (g)	12
Saturated fat (g)	7
Unsaturated fat (g)	4
Cholesterol (mg)	47
Sodium (mg)	219
Calories	277

 Makes
6 servings

CHOCOLATE-DIPPED FRUITS

Elegant sweets to serve with coffee. The chocolate dries to a brittle shell against the tender, tart-sweet fruit. The effect is deliciously sensual.

INGREDIENTS

6oz (180g) semisweet chocolate (see page 43)

½ pint (90g) fresh strawberries

½ cup (90g) dried apricots

¼lb (90g) fresh cherries, sweet if possible

½ cup (90g) dried pear halves

1 Melt the chocolate gently in a heatproof bowl over a pan of hot water. Dip the strawberries, apricots, and cherries in the melted chocolate so that they are coated on one half only. Let cool on waxed paper.

2 Cut the pear halves in half lengthwise. Dip the long inside edge of each piece in the melted chocolate and let cool on the paper.

3 Put the fruits in small paper cases, if desired. Store in an airtight container in the refrigerator until ready to use.

Per serving

Total fat (g)	9
Saturated fat (g)	5
Unsaturated fat (g)	4
Cholesterol (mg)	3
Sodium (mg)	9
Calories	222

 Makes
6 servings

WICKEDLY DECADENT DEEP CHOCOLATE TRUFFLES

These are a much lower-in-fat version of a frighteningly high-fat classic. The secret ingredient is fromage frais, mixed with the very best melted chocolate.

INGREDIENTS

6oz (180g) semisweet chocolate (see page 43)

6oz (180g) very low-fat fromage frais

about 2 tbsp confectioners' sugar

½ tsp vanilla extract

⅓oz (15g) semisweet chocolate, grated

1 Break the chocolate into a bowl over a pan of simmering water. Let it melt, stirring occasionally.

2 In a separate bowl, whisk together the fromage frais and sugar. Whisk in the vanilla.

3 When the chocolate is melted and smooth, remove from the heat and allow to cool slightly.

Slowly whisk the chocolate into the fromage frais mixture, using a rubber spatula to incorporate every bit of chocolate. Cover with plastic wrap and chill for an hour.

4 Line a baking sheet with waxed paper. Scatter the grated chocolate on a plate. Scoop out the chilled chocolate mixture in teaspoonfuls, roll into balls, then roll the balls in the grated chocolate and put on the prepared baking sheet. Cover with plastic wrap and refrigerate until firm.

5 Put the truffles in small paper cases. Store in an airtight container in the refrigerator until ready to use.

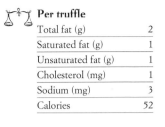

Per truffle

Total fat (g)	2
Saturated fat (g)	1
Unsaturated fat (g)	1
Cholesterol (mg)	1
Sodium (mg)	3
Calories	52

 Makes
24 truffles

FRUIT DESSERTS

FRUIT SALAD MAKES A STUNNING FINISH for a meal. It is a great blessing that it does so with such high nutritional value and such low fat content. The secret is to use the best fruit, at the perfect point of fragrant ripeness. Single fruit salads, like Cherries in Cointreau, Strawberries in Balsamic Vinegar, and peaches or nectarines with Crème de Pêche, orange juice, and vanilla, are dramatic, pure, and intense. Fruit can also be used in many other ways and is especially good with skim milk and low-fat dairy products. These ingredients may sound unadventurous, but in the guises they take on here, they are anything but.

MANGO COEUR A LA CREME

INGREDIENTS

For the coeur à la crème

1 large mango, cubed (see page 136)

13oz (400g) ricotta

4oz (125g) Quark (or use all ricotta, 17oz (525g) in all)

½–1 tbsp orange marmalade

few drops each orange and lemon juice

For the Mango Coulis

2 mangoes, about ¾lb (300g), cubed (see page 136)

confectioners' sugar, to taste

few drops of lemon juice (optional)

Romantic, colorful, and blissfully creamy, this heart-shaped dessert would be wonderful served with a few Almond Cookies for contrast (see page 148). It can also be made dome-shaped by draining it in a lined sieve – less romantic, but still colorful and creamy.

1 Line a large 2½ cup (600ml) coeur à la crème mold with a piece of damp cheesecloth. Set the mold in a shallow pie plate.

2 Put the mango, ricotta, and Quark in a food processor and process until smooth. Taste the mixture and add marmalade and the citrus juices to taste, although the dominant flavor should still be mango. Process well.

3 Pile the mixture into the mold, and flip over the edges of the cloth to cover. Let the mold, on the pie plate, drain in the refrigerator overnight.

4 For the Mango Coulis, puree the cubed mango in a food processor or blender. Sweeten to taste with the sugar, adding lemon juice if you wish to sharpen the taste a little.

5 To serve the coeur à la crème, unmold it onto a pretty plate. Surround with the Mango Coulis and serve with Tropical Fruit Salad (see page 136) or Strawberries in Lemon Balsamic Syrup (see page 128), if desired.

VARIATION

Serve the coeur à la crème with a raspberry coulis instead of the Mango Coulis. For a raspberry coulis, use two 12oz (375g) packages of frozen raspberries, thawed. Puree the fruit, then sieve it to eliminate the seeds. Add confectioners' sugar and lemon juice, as for the Mango Coulis.

Per serving	
Total fat (g)	6
Saturated fat (g)	4
Unsaturated fat (g)	2
Cholesterol (mg)	25
Sodium (mg)	59
Calories	132

Makes
1 large coeur à la crème or 8 individual ones

MANGO COEUR A LA CREME: *romance comes heart-shaped.*

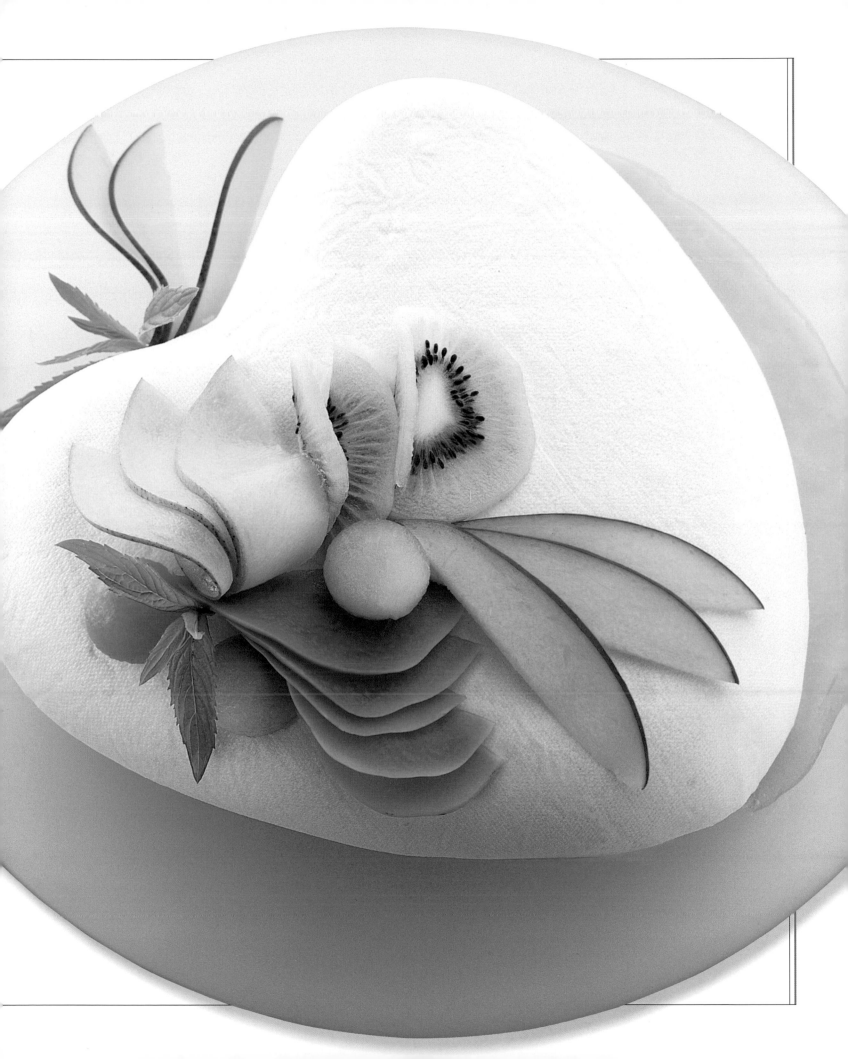

SWEET VERMOUTH-BATHED SUMMER PUDDING

*B*oth this Summer Pudding and the Winter Pudding (opposite) are splendidly healthy recipes – I love the idea of a bread-encased dome of packed fruits, the juices from the pressed fruits imbuing the bread with flavor and color. The wines in the puddings are simmered, so the alcohol evaporates, leaving flavor, but no alcohol calories.

INGREDIENTS

2lb (1kg) frozen summer fruits, thawed

2 cups (450ml) sweet vermouth

juice and zest of 1 large orange

4 tbsp lemon juice

zest of 1 large lemon

1in (2.5cm) piece of cinnamon stick

1 vanilla bean

2 tbsp sugar

7–8 thin slices white bread, 1–2 days old, crusts trimmed off

1 Put the thawed fruit in a colander over a bowl and press it down to extract even more juice. Set aside and reserve all juices.

2 Put the vermouth, citrus juices and zests, cinnamon, and vanilla bean in a saucepan and boil until reduced by a third. Stir in the sugar and reserved juice. Continue to boil, stirring, for 2–3 minutes. Remove from the heat, stir in the fruit, and let cool. Remove the cinnamon and vanilla bean.

3 Cut the bread diagonally into quarters. Use most of it to line the bottom and sides of a 3¾ cup (900ml) mixing bowl.

4 Put the fruit mixture in the bread-lined bowl. Cover the fruit with the remaining bread. Put a plate that fits in the bowl on top of the pudding. Place a large can on the plate to weight it. Put the pudding on a tray or plate to catch the overflow, then chill for at least 8 hours. Loosen the sides of the pudding and turn out onto a plate.

 Per serving

Total fat (g)	1
Saturated fat (g)	neg
Unsaturated fat (g)	1
Cholesterol (mg)	0
Sodium (mg)	140
Calories	135

 Makes
6 servings

SHERRY-SCENTED WINTER PUDDING

This winter version of Summer Pudding tastes fabulous made with a mixture of dried fruits such as apricots, apples, sour cherries, cranberries, figs, prunes, peaches, and pears.

INGREDIENTS

4 tbsp golden raisins

1lb (500g) mixed dried fruit, chopped into small pieces

grated rind and juice of 1 lemon

1½ cups (350ml) fresh orange juice

⅔ cup (150ml) cream sherry

1in (2.5cm) piece of cinnamon stick

1 tsp vanilla extract

4 tbsp Cointreau

1 tbsp apricot preserves

7–8 thin slices white bread, 1–2 days old, crusts trimmed off

1 Put all the ingredients except half the orange juice and all the bread in a skillet and simmer, stirring occasionally, until the fruits are plump and the liquid is almost gone. Be careful not to scorch it.

2 Cool the fruit mixture and remove the piece of cinnamon. Continue making the Winter Pudding according to steps 3 and 4 of the Summer Pudding (opposite), using the remaining orange juice to paint over any pale bits on the pudding when it is turned out.

Per serving

Total fat (g)	1
Saturated fat (g)	neg
Unsaturated fat (g)	1
Cholesterol (mg)	0
Sodium (mg)	200
Calories	361

Makes
6 servings

FRUIT RICOTTA TIRAMISU

Full-fat Tiramisù is a wicked combination of ingredients, including mascarpone cheese, egg yolks, and whipped cream. My "light" version is magnificent – you'll never miss the full-fat ingredients. Use cubes of Angel Cake (see page 143) in place of the ladyfingers to bring the fat count even lower.

INGREDIENTS

15–16 Italian ladyfingers

1 pint (250g) each strawberries, blueberries, raspberries

2 ripe peaches, cubed, juices reserved

1 tsp vanilla extract

2 tbsp fresh orange juice

1 tbsp orange liqueur

1lb 2oz (550g) ricotta

13oz (400g) Quark (if unavailable use all ricotta (1lb 15oz (950g) in total)

about 2 tbsp blueberry preserves

2 pairs amaretti

1 Line the bottom of a 12 x 7in (30 x 18cm) clear glass baking dish with a layer of ladyfingers.

2 Halve or quarter the strawberries and mix with all the berries in a bowl. Add the peach cubes, with their juice. Sprinkle with half the vanilla extract, the orange juice, and the liqueur. Toss with two spoons until thoroughly combined. Spread the fruit over the ladyfingers.

3 Put the ricotta and Quark in a food processor with the remaining vanilla extract and the blueberry preserves. Process until the mixture is smooth and fluffy.

4 Spread the cheese mixture smoothly over the fruit. Don't worry if some of the fruit shows through the cheese layer.

5 Using a kitchen mallet, crush the amaretti and sprinkle the crumbs evenly over the cheese layer. Cover with plastic wrap and chill for at least 2 hours before serving.

VARIATIONS

Try Cherries in Cointreau (see page 128) for the fruit layer and cherry preserves to flavor the "cream," then top with sieved confectioners' sugar and cocoa.

Use just the raspberries and strawberries, cover with a layer of Chocolate Cheesecake Mousse (see page 122), and top with ½oz (15g) grated semisweet chocolate.

Per serving

Total fat (g)	12
Saturated fat (g)	7
Unsaturated fat (g)	4
Cholesterol (mg)	47
Sodium (mg)	373
Calories	344

Makes
6 servings

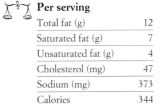

CHERRIES IN COINTREAU

I can never get enough of fresh cherries when they are – all too briefly – in season. For maximum cherriness, use a combination of all the varieties you can find.

INGREDIENTS

1¾lb (875g) cherries, halved and pitted

juice of 1½ oranges

4 tbsp lemon juice

slivered zest of ½ orange

slivered zest of ½ lemon

4 tbsp orange liqueur (e.g., Cointreau)

2 tsp vanilla extract

2–3 tbsp superfine sugar

Put all the ingredients in a bowl and mix together gently with two spoons. Cover with plastic wrap. Chill overnight in the refrigerator.

VARIATION

Replace the cherries with blood oranges, cut into wedges, or two or three navel oranges, peeled, all pith removed, and sliced into rings (not too thick).

 Per serving

Total fat (g)	neg
Saturated fat (g)	neg
Unsaturated fat (g)	neg
Cholesterol (mg)	0
Sodium (mg)	6
Calories	193

 Makes
4 servings

PEACH SALAD

The fragrance of vanilla with ripe peaches is magnificent. If you can't find Crème de Pêche, substitute Amaretto liqueur.

INGREDIENTS

6 large, ripe peaches

2–3 tbsp orange liqueur

1 tbsp Crème de Pêche

2 tsp vanilla extract

a few drops of lemon juice, to taste

pinch of sugar, to taste

1 Peel the peaches by putting them in a bowl of hot water for 30 seconds. Lift them out with a spoon, hold briefly under cold running water, then peel and slice.

2 Put the peaches and remaining ingredients in a bowl. Gently mix with two spoons. Omit the sugar if the peaches are very sweet.

VARIATION

Replace the peaches with ripe nectarines. Peeling is unnecessary.

 Per serving

Total fat (g)	neg
Saturated fat (g)	neg
Unsaturated fat (g)	neg
Cholesterol (mg)	0
Sodium (mg)	3
Calories	112

 Makes
4 servings

STRAWBERRIES IN LEMON BALSAMIC SYRUP

If you have never tried strawberries bathed in a syrup of balsamic vinegar and lemon juice, you are in for a treat. The amount of sugar depends on the quality of the vinegar, so taste as you go.

INGREDIENTS

¼ cup (60ml) lemon juice

1–2 tbsp sugar

1 tbsp balsamic vinegar

2 pints (475g) strawberries, hulled and quartered

Put the lemon juice in a bowl. Add the sugar, stir, and let sit until the sugar has dissolved. Stir in the balsamic vinegar. Toss the strawberries in the mixture until thoroughly combined. Let sit, stirring occasionally, until the strawberries are bathed in a syrupy sauce.

 Per serving

Total fat (g)	neg
Saturated fat (g)	neg
Unsaturated fat (g)	neg
Cholesterol (mg)	0
Sodium (mg)	8
Calories	55

 Makes
4 servings

CARAMELIZED PEARS

Pears in sweet vermouth are heavenly. I like to serve these folded in crepes, but they are also good as they are, topped with a Ricotta or Yogurt cream (see page 137), and served with an Almond Cookie or two (see page 148).

INGREDIENTS

1 orange

1 lemon

4 firm, ripe pears

1¼ cups (300ml) sweet vermouth

1 cinnamon stick

1 vanilla bean

½–1 tbsp superfine sugar

1 tbsp orange liqueur

1 Squeeze the juice of ½ lemon and ½ orange into a bowl. Peel the pears, and turn them in the citrus juices to prevent discoloration. Halve and core the pears, then dip them again. Dice the halves.

2 Put the diced pears in a heavy-bottomed skillet with the citrus juice from the bowl, the slivered zest of ¼ orange and ¼ lemon, the vermouth, cinnamon, vanilla bean, sugar, and liqueur.

3 Bring the pears and liquid to a boil and boil, uncovered, stirring frequently, until the pears are tender. With a skimmer or slotted spoon, lift the pears out of the pan, leaving the liquid in it, and put them in a bowl.

4 Discard the cinnamon and vanilla bean. Boil down the liquid in the pan until thickened and syrupy. Pour and scrape the liquid into a measuring cup.

5 Return the pears to the skillet, along with the juice of the remaining ½ lemon and ½ orange. Stir and cook quickly (but gently so that the pears do not break up) until the pears are richly glazed. Pour the sweet vermouth liquid back into the pan and stir together.

Per serving

Total fat (g)	1
Saturated fat (g)	neg
Unsaturated fat (g)	1
Cholesterol (mg)	0
Sodium (mg)	19
Calories	256

Makes
2 servings

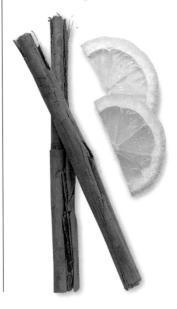

SWEET VERMOUTH SYRUP

A sophisticated dark ruby, spice and vanilla-scented sauce to serve with fruit such as pears, apricots, peaches, and oranges.

INGREDIENTS

one 25oz (75cl) bottle sweet vermouth

juice and slivered zest of 2 large oranges

juice and slivered zest of 2 large lemons

1 cinnamon stick

1 vanilla bean

1 cup (250ml) water

4–5 tbsp sugar

1 Put all the ingredients for the syrup, except the sugar, in a heavy-bottomed saucepan and bring to a boil. Boil rapidly, uncovered, until the liquid has reduced by about half.

2 Take the saucepan off the heat and stir in the sugar, making sure it is completely dissolved before returning the pan to the heat. Boil the syrup for 4–5 minutes more. Remove the pan from the heat and set aside to cool completely.

3 Transfer the syrup to a bowl, cover with plastic wrap, and chill in the refrigerator.

4 Remove the cinnamon stick and vanilla bean from the chilled syrup. Scrape out the pulp from the vanilla bean and stir it into the syrup. (Save the scraped bean for flavoring a jar of sugar to make vanilla sugar.)

Per tablespoon

Total fat (g)	neg
Saturated fat (g)	neg
Unsaturated fat (g)	neg
Cholesterol (mg)	0
Sodium (mg)	3
Calories	62

Makes
About 1¼ cups (300ml) or 20 tablespoons

BLUEBERRY COMPOTE

Any of these compotes can be used in other desserts or served as they are with a ricotta, yogurt, or fromage frais cream topping. They are also good with wedges of Angel Cake (see page 143).

INGREDIENTS

4 cups (500g) blueberries

2–3 tbsp blueberry preserves

1 tbsp cornstarch

juice of ½ lemon

1 tsp vanilla extract

1 Put the blueberries in a ceramic or glass baking dish. Blend all the other ingredients together until smooth and then mix with the blueberries in the baking dish.

2 Put the dish, uncovered, in a preheated oven and bake for about 15 minutes, stirring occasionally, until the mixture is thickened and bubbling.

3 Allow the compote to cool before serving.

  Per serving

Total fat (g)	neg
Saturated fat (g)	neg
Unsaturated fat (g)	neg
Cholesterol (mg)	0
Sodium (mg)	5
Calories	47

 Oven temperature
375°F/190°C

Makes
5 servings

PEACH COMPOTE

Another delicious compote, in which the sweetness of the fruit is balanced by the addition of a little citrus juice and zest. Nectarines could replace the peaches here.

INGREDIENTS

1¼lb (875g) peaches, unpeeled

2 tbsp superfine sugar

1 tbsp cornstarch

2 tbsp fresh orange juice

slivered zest of ½ small lemon

slivered zest of ½ small orange

½ tsp vanilla extract

pinch of salt

1 Pit the peaches and cut into chunks over a bowl so that you catch all the juice. Put them and the juice with the other ingredients in a heavy-bottomed stainless steel or ceramic saucepan.

2 Cook slowly until the liquid is thick and syrupy. The fruit should be tender, but still retain its shape. Cool the compote before serving.

 Per serving

Total fat (g)	neg
Saturated fat (g)	neg
Unsaturated fat (g)	neg
Cholesterol (mg)	0
Sodium (mg)	42
Calories	88

 Makes
5 servings

PLUM-PEACH COMPOTE

INGREDIENTS

1¼lb (625g) peaches, unpeeled

1¾lb (875g) plums, unpeeled

1 scant tbsp cornstarch

4–5 tbsp light brown sugar

slivered zest of ½ lemon and ½ orange

1 tsp vanilla extract

3 tbsp fresh orange juice

pinch of salt

1 Pit the peaches and plums and cut into chunks over a bowl to catch the juice. Put the fruits and their juice in a heavy-bottomed stainless steel or ceramic saucepan.

2 Add the cornstarch, sugar, citrus zest, vanilla, orange juice, and salt. Cook slowly, stirring, until the fruit is tender but still keeps its shape. Let cool.

VARIATION

For an apricot and peach compote, use 1¾lb (875g) unpeeled apricots and 10oz (300g) unpeeled peaches in place of the peaches and plums, and 1 tablespoon Amaretto di Saronno in place of the fresh orange juice.

 Per serving

Total fat (g)	neg
Saturated fat (g)	neg
Unsaturated fat (g)	neg
Cholesterol (mg)	0
Sodium (mg)	46
Calories	162

 Makes
5 servings

CLAFOUTIS

This sumptuous dessert delivers all the satisfaction of a fruit pie – with hardly any fat at all. The clafoutis, puffed up as it emerges from the oven, subsides a little as it cools. Serve it hot, warm, or at room temperature.

INGREDIENTS

oil-water spray (for the tart pan)

For the batter

1 cup (105g) all-purpose flour

½ cup (105g) light brown sugar

3 tbsp skim milk powder

pinch of freshly grated nutmeg

1¼ cups (300ml) skim milk

6 tbsp low-fat plain yogurt

4 egg whites

2 tsp vanilla extract

For the fruit mixture

1¼lb (625g) peaches, pitted and cut into chunks, any juice reserved

2–3 tbsp sugar

2 tbsp orange juice

few drops of lemon juice

1 tbsp apricot preserves, melted

1 For the batter, sift the flour, sugar, milk powder, and nutmeg into a bowl. Whisk together the milk, yogurt, egg whites, and vanilla. Pour into the flour mixture and beat or whisk until smooth. Pour the batter into the prepared pan.

2 For the fruit mixture, mix together the peaches and any juices, the sugar, and the citrus juices. Scatter the mixture over the batter, leaving a 1in (2.5cm) border all around.

3 Bake in a preheated oven for 30–40 minutes, until set, lightly browned, and puffed. When it starts to puff and bubble, quickly and gently brush apricot preserves around the edges. Remove from the oven and set it on a wire rack.

VARIATIONS

Use nectarines instead of peaches, or a mixture of halved, pitted cherries and apricots, pitted and cut into chunks, or wedges of tart eating apples and raisins.

 Per serving

Total fat (g)	1
Saturated fat (g)	0
Unsaturated fat (g)	1
Cholesterol (mg)	2
Sodium (mg)	121
Calories	240

 Oven temperature
375°F/190°C

 Baking time
30–40 minutes

 Baking pan
10in (25cm) nonstick tart pan, lightly oil-water sprayed

 Makes
6 servings

RICE PUDDING WITH GOLDEN RAISINS

This amazing rice pudding is virtually fat-free, yet it tastes so fattening! It bakes long and slow so the sugar and milk sugars caramelize – this is part of what gives the pudding its flavor and richness.

INGREDIENTS

6 tbsp golden raisins

⅓ cup (90ml) Cointreau

2 tbsp superfine sugar

5 cups (1.2 liters) skim milk, at room temperature

1 tsp vanilla extract

6 heaping tbsp skim milk powder

¾ cup (125g) arborio rice

1 Put the golden raisins and Cointreau in a bowl; let soak.

2 Meanwhile, thoroughly mix together the sugar, milk, vanilla, and milk powder. Stir in the rice, then add the golden raisins and Cointreau.

3 Pour the mixture into a 9in (23cm) square baking dish and set the dish in a bain marie (a roasting pan is fine). Pour boiling water into the pan so that it comes two thirds of the way up the sides.

4 Bake in a preheated oven for about 2¼ hours, stirring after each 20–30 minutes, until the rice is tender and bathed in a thick, creamy sauce. Serve the pudding warm or cold, sprinkled with cinnamon or nutmeg, if desired.

 Per serving

Total fat (g)	2
Saturated fat (g)	1
Unsaturated fat (g)	1
Cholesterol (mg)	8
Sodium (mg)	264
Calories	432

 Oven temperature
300°F/150°C

 Baking time
about 2¼ hours

 Makes
4 servings

BLUEBERRY AMARETTI CRUMBLE

These elegant yet homey classics taste extremely indulgent, even though they are very low in sugar and fat. I love serving them warm, with a dollop of Cream Topping, flavored with an appropriate fruit preserve (see page 137).

INGREDIENTS

4 cups (500g) blueberries

3–4 tbsp superfine sugar

1 tbsp cornstarch

½ tsp vanilla extract

½ tbsp lemon juice

juice of ½ orange

pinch each cinnamon and nutmeg

6 pairs amaretti cookies

1 cup (90g) Grape Nuts® cereal

1 whole egg

2 egg whites

1 Mix together in a glass bowl the blueberries, sugar, cornstarch, vanilla, lemon and orange juices, cinnamon, and nutmeg. Taste, and add more sugar, if necessary.

2 Put the mixture in a glass or ceramic baking dish and bake, uncovered, in a preheated oven for 15 minutes, until thick, bubbly, and juicy. Take the blueberries out of the oven and raise the oven temperature to the higher setting.

3 Put the amaretti cookies and cereal in a food processor and process until they are coarse crumbs. Add the egg and whites and process until well mixed. Spread the mixture evenly over the blueberries, leaving a ½in (1cm) border all around.

4 Return the baking dish to the oven and bake for 7–10 minutes longer, until the topping is set and the juices are bubbling. Serve warm or cold.

 Per serving

Total fat (g)	2
Saturated fat (g)	<1
Unsaturated fat (g)	1
Cholesterol (mg)	32
Sodium (mg)	143
Calories	177

 Oven temperature
375°F/190°C, then 400°F/200°C

 Baking time
22–25 minutes

 Makes
6 servings

PEACH AMARETTI CRUMBLE

My two favorite fruits for crumbles are peach and blueberry, but apple, pear, cherry, apricot, or nectarine are good too. Amaretti cookies contain no fat or oil: the almond flavor is derived from apricot pits, not high-fat almonds. Illustrated opposite.

INGREDIENTS

juice of ½ orange

1 tbsp peach preserves

1 tbsp Crème de Peche or Cointreau

1 tbsp Amaretto di Saronno

1 tsp vanilla extract

1 tbsp cornstarch

5–6 peaches (1½lb/750g), peeled (see page 128) and sliced

6 pairs amaretti cookies

1 cup (90g) Grape Nuts® cereal

1 whole egg

2 egg whites

1 Put the orange juice, peach preserves, liqueurs, vanilla, and cornstarch in a shallow baking dish, making sure the cornstarch is mixed in smoothly. Add the peach slices. Toss gently with two spoons to coat the peach slices in the mixture. Bake, uncovered, in a preheated oven for 15 minutes, until bubbling.

2 Put the amaretti cookies and cereal in a food processor and process to fine crumbs. Add the egg and the whites. Process until well mixed, then spread evenly over the peaches, leaving a ½in (1cm) border all around.

3 Raise the oven temperature to the higher setting and bake the crumble for 7–10 minutes longer, until the top is set and the juices are bubbling.

4 Serve the crumble warm. It is delicious with fruit-flavored Cream Topping; choose apricot or peach preserves for the flavoring (see page 137).

 Per serving

Total fat (g)	2
Saturated fat (g)	<1
Unsaturated fat (g)	1
Cholesterol (mg)	32
Sodium (mg)	142
Calories	174

 Oven temperature
375°F/190°C, then 400°F/200°C

 Baking time
22–25 minutes

 Makes
6 servings

RASPBERRY ALMOND CREAM TRIFLE

A trifle is such an extravagant concoction, ideal for feeding a large gathering. To make this trifle even lower in fat, replace the ladyfingers with cubes of Angel Cake (see page 143). Adding a jelly layer to a trifle is a relatively new idea; when the jelly is a fresh fruit and sherry one, I like it very much.

INGREDIENTS

For the cake layer

12 ladyfingers or cubed sponge cake

For the raspberry jelly

1lb (500g) frozen raspberries, thawed, and juice reserved

2 envelopes (1 tbsp each) gelatin

1 cup (250ml) orange juice

½ cup (100g) sugar

1 cup (250ml) medium sherry

For the creamy almond layer

2 cups (500ml) skim milk

¼ cup (45g) skim milk powder

¼ tsp almond extract

1 envelope (1 tbsp) gelatin

½ cup (125ml) hot water

pinch of salt

½ cup (125g) sugar

1lb (500g) very low-fat fromage frais

For the honeyed vanilla cream topping

1 vanilla bean

1lb (500g) very low-fat fromage frais

2 tbsp honey

1 For the cake layer, arrange the ladyfingers in a single layer on the bottom of a large, clear glass bowl, cutting to make them fit.

2 For the jelly, put the reserved juice from the defrosted berries in a measuring cup. If necessary, add enough water to make 1½ cups (350ml). Put the liquid in a saucepan and heat it. Sprinkle in the gelatin and let soften.

3 Bring the orange juice to a boil in a small pan and add it and the sugar to the liquid in the saucepan, stirring until the sugar has dissolved completely. Stir in the sherry. Cool slightly, then stir in the raspberries. Let come to room temperature.

4 Pour the mixture over the ladyfingers, soaking them. Chill until completely set: this will take several hours.

5 For the creamy almond layer, whisk together the milk and milk powder. Rinse a heavy-bottomed nonstick saucepan and pour out the water, but do not dry it. Put the whisked milk and almond extract in the pan and bring to just below boiling. Meanwhile, sprinkle the gelatin over the hot water; let soften.

6 When the milk is just forming bubbles on the edges, add the salt and sugar and stir until dissolved. Whisk in the softened gelatin; cool to lukewarm.

7 Whisk the fromage frais and the milk mixture together, then rub the mixture through a sieve into a bowl. Pour this mixture over the firmly set jelly. Chill for several hours until the creamy almond layer is set.

TO MAKE THE TOPPING

1 For the topping, take a small, sharp knife and split the vanilla bean lengthwise. Scrape the soft pulp from each half into the fromage frais.

2 Whisk the honey into the fromage frais and stir until the black vanilla bean seeds are evenly distributed.

3 Swirl the cream topping over the set custard. Decorate with thawed frozen raspberries and mandarin orange segments, if desired, before serving.

 Per serving

Total fat (g)	1
Saturated fat (g)	<1
Unsaturated fat (g)	<1
Cholesterol (mg)	3
Sodium (mg)	163
Calories	353

 Makes
8 servings

MERINGUE LAYER TORTE

The fillings and toppings in this meringue layer torte can be endlessly varied using other recipes in this book. For small meringues, like those used in the Meringue Stack (see above and page 14), pipe 3in (7cm) circles of the mixture and bake for one hour only.

INGREDIENTS

For the meringue layers

5 egg whites, at room temperature

pinch of cream of tartar

pinch of salt

1 cup (200g) superfine sugar

1 tsp vanilla extract

For the fillings

1 batch of Chocolate Cheesecake Mousse, undrained (see page 122)

½ batch of cherry Cream Topping (see page 137)

4oz (125g) Cherries in Cointreau, drained (see page 128)

1 For the meringue layers, beat the egg whites with the cream of tartar and salt in a bowl until foamy. Beat in the sugar, 1–2 tablespoons at a time, until the mixture is shiny and stiff and holds firm peaks. Fold in the vanilla.

2 Line 3 baking sheets with baking parchment. Trace an 8in (20cm) circle on each. Pipe the meringue mixture to fill each circle. Bake in a preheated oven for 3 hours. Leave in the switched-off oven to cool thoroughly (at least 3 hours).

3 To assemble, spread one meringue disk with Chocolate Cheesecake Mousse. Top with a second disk and spread with cherry Cream Topping. Add the last meringue disk and spread with the mousse. Top with Cherries in Cointreau.

Per serving

Total fat (g)	14
Saturated fat (g)	9
Unsaturated fat (g)	5
Cholesterol (mg)	60
Sodium (mg)	366
Calories	508

Oven temperature
225°F/110°C

Baking time
3 hours

Makes
6 servings

MANGO MILLEFEUILLE WITH TROPICAL FRUIT SALAD

This is a very elegant dessert, with phyllo pastry forming the leaves of the millefeuille. Commercial oil spray (still very low-fat) is needed here – my oil-water spray would make the pastry soggy. The mango cream filling is one of my favorites.

INGREDIENTS

For the pastry

10oz (300g) frozen phyllo pastry, thawed

commercial oil spray

For the mango cream

2 large mangoes (about 1lb (500g) each), cubed (see below)

9oz (275g) ricotta

4oz (125g) Quark (if unavailable, use all ricotta, 13oz (400g) in total recipe)

½–1 tbsp orange marmalade

1 tsp vanilla extract

For the tropical fruit salad

2 or 3 pieces tropical fruit, such as papaya, melon, and pineapple, cubed

2 blood oranges, cubed, juice reserved

1 kiwi, sliced

dash or two of vanilla extract

dash of Crème de Peche

dash of Cointreau

1 Unroll the pastry. Using a 3in (7cm) diameter glass as a guide, cut eight circles from the stack of phyllo with a knife. Each circular stack will have about 8 sheets of pastry. Cover with plastic wrap.

2 Oil-spray a nonstick baking sheet. Take one stack of phyllo leaves, separate the layers, and stack them, one on top of the other, on the baking sheet. Spray each one lightly with oil spray as you do so. Repeat with the remaining stacks.

3 Bake in a preheated oven for 5–8 minutes, until browned and a bit crisp. Flip the stacks over about halfway through the baking time. Cool on a wire rack.

4 For the mango cream, put half the mango cubes, the ricotta, Quark, orange marmalade to taste, and vanilla in a food processor. Process until smooth and creamy.

5 For the tropical fruit salad, mix the remaining mango with the other ingredients. Cover with plastic wrap and macerate for an hour or so in the refrigerator.

6 To serve, put one stack of phyllo circles on a plate. Cover with mango cream and top with another phyllo stack. Finish with tropical fruit salad and decorate with sprigs of fresh mint, if desired.

Per serving	
Total fat (g)	10
Saturated fat (g)	5
Unsaturated fat (g)	5
Cholesterol (mg)	35
Sodium (mg)	244
Calories	508

Oven temperature
400°F/200°C

Baking time
5–8 minutes

Makes
4 servings

TO PEEL AND CUBE A MANGO

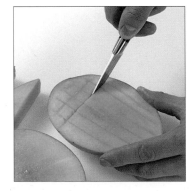

1 Cut the mango lengthwise in half, down one side of the pit. Slice down again on the other side of the pit.

2 Set aside the mango halves. Peel the skin from the flat center section, slice the flesh off the pit, and cut into cubes.

3 Score each mango half lengthwise and crosswise, cutting all the way to, but not through, the skin.

4 Push out the skin as if you were pushing the half-mango inside out and cut the cubes off the skins.

YOGURT CREAM TOPPING

These three toppings really rival whipped cream – they are luscious, creamy, yet low in fat. The magic ingredients are Quark, fromage frais, very low-fat yogurt (all 0% fat), and ricotta (15% fat).

INGREDIENTS

2 cups (500g) low-fat yogurt

1 tbsp honey, to taste

2 tsp vanilla extract, or the pulp of a vanilla bean

1 Drain the yogurt overnight in a sieve lined with cheesecloth. The yogurt will lose about half its volume.

2 Whisk in the honey to taste, then the vanilla extract or pulp.

 Per serving

Total fat (g)	1
Saturated fat (g)	0.5
Unsaturated fat (g)	0.5
Cholesterol (mg)	3
Sodium (mg)	183
Calories	124

Makes
2 servings

YOGURT "WHIPPED CREAM"

This is my only recipe that uses uncooked egg whites and I always issue the following warning: do not feed it to pregnant women, small children, the elderly, or the infirm.

INGREDIENTS

1 cup (250g) low-fat yogurt, drained (see Yogurt Cream Topping, above)

¼ tsp vanilla extract

2 egg whites, at room temperature

pinch of cream of tartar

2 tbsp superfine sugar

1 Stir together the yogurt and vanilla extract.

2 In a spotlessly clean bowl, whisk the egg whites with the cream of tartar until foamy.

3 Add the sugar, a little at a time, and continue beating until the egg whites are shiny and hold firm peaks.

4 Fold the beaten egg whites gently into the yogurt mixture, and use immediately.

 Per serving

Total fat (g)	neg
Saturated fat (g)	neg
Unsaturated fat (g)	neg
Cholesterol (mg)	1
Sodium (mg)	59
Calories	49

Makes
5 servings

RICOTTA CREAM TOPPING

This lusciously creamy topping can be made with all ricotta, or ricotta combined with Quark or fromage frais. Use marmalade, preserves, or jam instead of sugar for a wonderfully subtle flavor. Wild blueberry preserves will tint the cream a misty lilac – sheer delight.

INGREDIENTS

1lb 2oz (560g) ricotta, or half ricotta, half fromage frais, or Quark

about 2 tbsp fruit preserves, marmalade, or jam

1 tsp vanilla extract

Put all the ingredients in a food processor and use the pulse button to blend them together. Fruit preserves or jam give a much better flavor and texture to the topping than does sugar.

VARIATIONS

For a chocolate cream topping, replace the preserves with 1 tablespoon each sifted low-fat cocoa and confectioners' sugar.

Depending on the preserves, the topping can take on a most intriguing color. Cherry imparts a rosy blush, blueberry turns it a hazy, misty lilac – quite enchanting! Orange marmalade (for an orange-flavored topping) gives a creamy orange color.

 Per serving

Total fat (g)	7
Saturated fat (g)	4
Unsaturated fat (g)	3
Cholesterol (mg)	32
Sodium (mg)	91
Calories	144
(based on ½ ricotta, ½ Quark)	

 Makes
4 servings

ICE CREAMS & SORBETS

INSTANT SORBETS AND ICE CREAMS are great fun to make and wonderfully nutritious to eat. Use pieces of frozen fruits to make sorbets, add buttermilk or fromage frais to make ice creams. There is a terrific variety of sorbets here, and the chocolate sorbet is a real stunner. For the ultimate chocolate experience, however, the Deep Chocolate Ice Cream, based on a hot fudge sauce, is pure indulgence. Low-fat ice creams can also be made with different varieties of fruit or fruit combinations, and the possibilities for flavoring frozen yogurt, as a delicious alternative to ice cream, are endless.

FRUITS FOR SORBETS

Sorbets made with sweeter fruits, such as mango or papaya, only need lemon juice to sharpen the flavor, but others will need sweetening. To sweeten a sorbet, choose a preserve or marmalade that matches or complements the flavor of the fruit. Berries or cubes of fresh fruit should be frozen flat in a single layer on trays, and then stored in plastic freezer bags until needed. Drop sharply on the counter to separate the pieces.

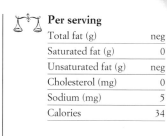

PAPAYA   BANANA   PEACH   STRAWBERRY

RASPBERRY BLUEBERRY SORBET

Countless variations on this sorbet are possible by changing the fruit and flavorings. For well-rounded flavor, I use honey or marmalades, preserves, or jams as sweeteners – they give so much more than just sweetness.

INGREDIENTS

2 cups (250g) frozen mixed blueberries and raspberries

2–3 tbsp orange juice

about 1 tbsp blueberry preserves

a few drops of lemon juice

1 Put the frozen blueberries and raspberries in a food processor with 1 tablespoon of the orange juice and the blueberry preserves. Process the mixture thoroughly until it is smooth and creamy. If there are any ice crystals remaining, process a little longer until they disappear.

2 Add more orange juice as needed to form a creamy consistency, along with the lemon juice and a little more preserves, if necessary. Stop processing to scrape down the sides occasionally. Serve at once.

VARIATIONS

For different yet equally delicious sorbets, replace the blueberries and raspberries with frozen sliced peaches or nectarines, pears, strawberries, or bananas. To make a wonderfully smooth ice cream, use fromage frais or buttermilk instead of orange juice.

 Per serving

Total fat (g)	neg
Saturated fat (g)	0
Unsaturated fat (g)	neg
Cholesterol (mg)	0
Sodium (mg)	5
Calories	34

Makes
2 servings

SORBETS WITH FRUIT OR CHOCOLATE *end a meal on a note of palate-tingling freshness.*

MANGO SORBET

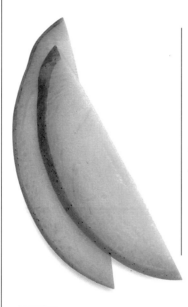

INGREDIENTS

8oz (250g) frozen mango cubes (see page 138)

a few drops of lemon juice, if necessary

1 Frozen mango whips up to a voluptuous creaminess, with virtually no added liquid. Put the frozen mango cubes in a food processor. Process until smooth and creamy, stopping to scrape down the sides when needed.

2 Taste, and if necessary add a few drops of lemon juice to sharpen the flavor. Spoon the sorbet into goblets and serve immediately.

VARIATION

Pineapple and Papaya Sorbet: replace the frozen mango cubes with 4oz (125g) frozen pineapple cubes and 4oz (125g) frozen papaya cubes.

 Per serving

Total fat (g)	neg
Saturated fat (g)	neg
Unsaturated fat (g)	neg
Cholesterol (mg)	0
Sodium (mg)	2
Calories	48

 Makes
3 servings

CHOCOLATE SORBET

Serious chocolate for serious chocoholics! This sorbet uses low-fat cocoa powder, and the ice cream (below) contains low-fat cocoa powder plus semisweet chocolate to ensure the maximum chocolate experience with a minimum of fat.

INGREDIENTS

1 cup (250g) superfine sugar

2¼ cups (575ml) water

½ cup (60g) low-fat cocoa powder (see page 43)

½ tsp vanilla extract

1 Gently heat the sugar and water in a heavy-bottomed pan until the sugar has dissolved. Bring to a boil, and continue to boil for 1 minute. Remove from the heat and allow to cool slightly.

2 Put the cocoa in a bowl and stir in a little cooled syrup to make a smooth paste. Gradually stir in the remaining syrup until all the cocoa is incorporated. Stir in the vanilla and strain through a fine sieve. Set aside to cool.

3 Freeze the mixture in an ice cream maker, following the manufacturer's instructions, or pour into a plastic container and freeze until slushy, then process in a food processor until fluffy and store in the freezer.

 Per serving

Total fat (g)	1
Saturated fat (g)	1
Unsaturated fat (g)	neg
Cholesterol (mg)	0
Sodium (mg)	95
Calories	185

 Makes
6 servings

DEEP CHOCOLATE ICE CREAM

Chocolate lovers take note: this is a deep, meaningful, chocolate experience. To call it intensely chocolaty does not begin to describe its impact. Like the sorbet above, this ice cream is best made in an ice cream maker, although it could also be made in the freezer.

INGREDIENTS

1¼ cups (275g) ricotta

1 cup (250ml) skim milk

For the Hot Fudge Base

6 tbsp low-fat cocoa powder

½ cup (100g) superfine sugar

8 tbsp nonfat milk powder

½ cup (125ml) cold water

1 tsp vanilla extract

½oz (15g) semisweet chocolate, grated

1 For the base, sift together the cocoa, sugar, and milk powder. Add the water, vanilla, and chocolate and mix to a smooth paste. Heat slowly, stirring, until bubbling gently. Let cool.

2 Process the ricotta and milk until smooth. Add the sauce and process again. Freeze in an ice cream maker, or freeze in a freezer, process until smooth, then refreeze (see Chocolate Sorbet, above).

 Per serving

Total fat (g)	5
Saturated fat (g)	3
Unsaturated fat (g)	2
Cholesterol (mg)	20
Sodium (mg)	187
Calories	183

Makes
8 servings

FROZEN STRAWBERRY YOGURT

If you make the instant food processor sorbet with honeyed Yogurt Cream, the result is this splendidly fruity frozen yogurt.

INGREDIENTS

2 cups (250–275g) frozen strawberry pieces (see page 138)

about 3 tbsp Yogurt Cream Topping (see page 137)

1 tsp vanilla extract

a few drops of lemon and orange juice

a drizzle of honey, optional

1 Put the frozen strawberry pieces in a food processor and process until slightly broken up.

2 Add 1 tablespoon of the Yogurt Cream Topping, then all the vanilla, and process until it forms a lumpy consistency.

3 With the machine still running, add another 1–2 tablespoons of Yogurt Cream Topping, and a few drops of orange and lemon juice, according to the tartness or sweetness of the strawberries. Add a drizzle of honey, if desired.

4 When the mixture forms a beautifully creamy, fluffy ice cream consistency, with no ice crystals, it is ready. Serve at once.

VARIATION

Experiment with different frozen fruits (see page 138) such as blueberry, banana, pineapple, peach, or papaya.

 Per serving

Total fat (g)	neg
Saturated fat (g)	neg
Unsaturated fat (g)	neg
Cholesterol (mg)	neg
Sodium (mg)	16
Calories	32

 Makes
3 servings

BANANA STRAWBERRY SMOOTHIE

These amazing milk drinks are marvelously nutritious, rich, and satisfying, yet they contain virtually no fat. Strictly speaking, they are not drinks because they must be eaten with a spoon. They are more of a cross between an old-fashioned soda fountain milkshake and whipped cream than a smoothie.

INGREDIENTS

1¼ cups (300ml) frozen skim milk

½ tsp vanilla extract

1 tbsp skim milk powder

1–2 tsp honey

frozen slices of 1 banana (see page 138)

4 large frozen strawberries, quartered

1 Partially thaw the skim milk (quick and easy in the microwave), until it becomes frozen slush.

2 Put the slush in a food processor (not a blender) with the milk powder and vanilla. Process until thickened and more than doubled in quantity. Drizzle in the honey.

3 Using scissors, chop the frozen banana slices in two and dice the frozen strawberry quarters.

4 With the food processor running, add the fruit pieces, a few at a time, until well pureed.

5 Pile the creamy mixture into two tall glasses, and "drink" it with a spoon.

VARIATIONS

Mango Smoothie: substitute frozen mango cubes (see page 138) for the banana and strawberries. These drinks can also be made with other fruits, or in chocolate or mocha versions (see below).

Chocolate Smoothie: omit the fruit and add 1–1½ tablespoons low-fat cocoa powder in Step 1. Add more honey, to taste.

Mocha Smoothie: omit the fruit. Add a sprinkling of low-fat cocoa powder, ¼–½ teaspoon instant espresso granules, and more honey to taste.

 Per serving

Total fat (g)	<1
Saturated fat (g)	<1
Unsaturated fat (g)	neg
Cholesterol (mg)	4
Sodium (mg)	127
Calories	138

 **Makes**
2 servings

BAKING

THE MOST OLD-FASHIONED AND EVOCATIVE of kitchen activities, baking fills the house with warmth, tantalizing fragrance, and happiness. Baking is deeply, viscerally satisfying, and bread is a cinch to make without fat. Even splendidly rich-looking cakes can be achieved with no fat at all, not even an egg yolk.

The Angel Cake here, which is made with egg whites, is the obvious no-fat classic in this collection, but there is also a mouthwatering Carrot Cranberry Loaf to tempt the palate as well as a rich Banana and Chocolate Loaf. Both of these loaves deliver sweet satisfaction without the fat.

CASSATA *extravagantly layers light-as-air cake, creamy filling, and candied peel.*

ANGEL CAKE

Even so-called fat-free sponge cakes are not no-fat cakes – they are made with whole eggs – but this Angel Cake is completely fat-free. It has an ethereal, delicate quality and is best served with berries and coulis or with fruit compotes. For a chocolate version, simply replace ¼ cup (30g) of the flour with 6 tablespoons low-fat cocoa powder.

INGREDIENTS

1 cup (125g) cake flour

1¼ cups plus 1 tbsp (275g) superfine sugar

10 egg whites, at room temperature

pinch of cream of tartar

1½ tsp vanilla extract

1 Sift together the flour and ½ cup (105g) of sugar and set aside.

2 Beat the egg whites until foamy, add the cream of tartar, and beat until they hold soft peaks. Continue beating, adding the remaining sugar, 2 tablespoons at a time, until the whites are stiff and glossy. Fold in the vanilla extract.

3 Sprinkle the flour mixture over the batter a little at a time and fold in gently but thoroughly.

4 Spoon the mixture into an ungreased 10in (25cm) tube pan. Bake in a preheated oven for 35–40 minutes, or until a cake tester inserted in the center comes out clean. The top of the cake will probably crack like a soufflé.

5 Invert the cake, in its pan, on an upright bottle or inverted funnel. Let cool for at least 1 hour.

6 Gently loosen the cake in the pan and slide it out onto a plate. Cut the cake into slices to serve, with a coulis or compote.

Per slice

Total fat (g)	neg
Saturated fat (g)	0
Unsaturated fat (g)	neg
Cholesterol (mg)	0
Sodium (mg)	48
Calories	135

Oven temperature
375°F/190°C

Baking time
35–40 minutes

Makes
12 slices

CASSATA

The three layers that make up this cake are cut from a delicate Angel Cake, baked flat rather than in a tube pan. As with all the recipes in this collection, there is no compromise here – this is a fabulous cake.

INGREDIENTS

For the cake

½ quantity Angel Cake mixture (see above)

For the filling and icing

⅔ cup (150ml) orange liqueur or Amaretto di Saronno

1 quantity orange Cream Topping (see page 137)

½ cup (90g) candied mixed peel, chopped

½ quantity Mocha Icing (see Dark Chocolate Icing, page 121)

1 Line a 13 x 9in (33 x 23cm) jelly roll pan or shallow baking sheet with baking parchment.

2 Make the cake mixture as for Angel Cake, following steps 1–3 above, and spread it into the prepared pan. Bake in a preheated oven for 15–18 minutes. Let the cake cool in the pan on a wire rack.

TO ASSEMBLE THE CAKE

1 Line a 9 x 5¾ x 2¾in (1kg) loaf pan with nonstick baking parchment, leaving an overlap at the top. Cut the cooled cake into thirds. Brush some of the liqueur over the top of each piece.

2 Put one piece of the cake, liqueur side up, in the loaf pan. Spread with half the orange Cream Topping and sprinkle half the candied peel. Repeat with a second piece of cake and the remaining Cream Topping and candied peel.

3 Top with the last piece of cake, liqueur side down, and pull the parchment up over the cake. Chill for at least 1 hour, or overnight.

4 Unwrap the cake, invert onto a serving plate, and ice with the Mocha Icing, reserving some for piping a decoration on top of the Cassata, if desired.

Per slice

Total fat (g)	4
Saturated fat (g)	2
Unsaturated fat (g)	2
Cholesterol (mg)	15
Sodium (mg)	171
Calories	278

Oven temperature
350°F/180°C

Baking time
15–18 minutes

Makes
10 slices

BASIC YEAST BREAD

This yeast bread is very easy to make, and the finished loaf has a delicious, crunchy bottom. It also makes an excellent pizza base (see page 145).

INGREDIENTS

4–5 cups (500–625g) unbleached flour (see method)

1 envelope fast-acting dry yeast

1½ tsp salt

about 1¼ cups (400ml) warm water

skim milk or lightly beaten egg white, to brush the top (optional)

1 Put 4 cups (500g) flour, the yeast, and salt in a large bowl and mix with your fingers. Pour in the warm water, stirring constantly with a wooden spoon. When the mixture forms a cohesive mass, begin kneading in the bowl, and sprinkle in the remaining flour, a little at a time, to make a malleable dough. The amount of additional flour the dough will absorb depends on the humidity and the quality of the flour.

2 Sprinkle some flour on a work surface and turn out the dough. Knead rhythmically, dusting with more flour as needed, until you have a smooth, pliable, not too sticky dough. It should be elastic and extremely responsive. Press the dough with your finger – if it springs back, it is ready.

3 Form the dough into a ball and let it rest. Wash and dry the mixing bowl. If using an electric oven, bring water to a boil.

4 Knead the dough briefly. Lightly flour a mixing bowl and put the dough in. Dust the top of the dough with flour and cover the bowl with plastic wrap. Put the bowl into the unlit oven. If using a gas oven, the pilot light will provide a warm environment for the dough to rise, but leave the oven door slightly ajar. If using an electric oven, set a roasting pan of boiling water on the oven floor and close the oven door. Leave for about 1 hour, until doubled in size.

5 Gently indent the dough with your finger and leave for 5–10 minutes. If the dent remains, the dough is ready for the next step.

6 Punch down the dough with your knuckles. Knead briefly and let it rest. Preheat the oven.

7 Sprinkle a nonstick baking sheet with flour or with cornmeal for a crunchy bottom on the bread. Cut the dough in half, knead each piece and nudge into a large oval shape, or flatten the oval out, then roll up into a baguette shape. Put the loaves on the baking sheet and make three slashes across the tops with a knife. Cover with a dish towel. Leave in a warm, draft-free place for 20–30 minutes, until doubled in size.

8 Uncover the loaves. Brush with milk or egg white to glaze. Don't let egg drip onto the baking sheet. For really crusty loaves, omit the glaze and spray the loaves with water two or three times during the first 10 minutes of baking.

9 If used, refill the pan on the bottom of the oven with boiling water. Bake the loaves for 40–50 minutes. When they are almost done, place them directly on the oven rack. If they appear to be browning too much on top, turn them upside down for the last few minutes. The bread is done when it is golden brown and sounds hollow when the bottom is tapped. Let cool on a wire rack.

Per loaf

Total fat (g)	4
Saturated fat (g)	1
Unsaturated fat (g)	3
Cholesterol (mg)	0
Sodium (mg)	981
Calories	960

Oven temperature
400°F/200°C

Baking time
40–30 minutes

Makes
2 x ¾lb (350g) loaves

MUSHROOM & PESTO PIZZA

SAUSAGE & CREAMY SPINACH PIZZA

TOMATO & MOZZARELLA PIZZAS

Tomato sauce and grated mozzarella cheese are classic toppings for pizza, but so is tomato sauce with no cheese or, for that matter, cheese with no tomato sauce. Add whatever you like: strips of well-trimmed prosciutto; grilled zucchini, peppers, and/or eggplant; crumbled meatballs or cooked fresh spinach; or pan-braised garlic cloves – whatever strikes your fancy.

TOMATO & RED
ONION PIZZA

INGREDIENTS

For the base

*1 quantity Basic Yeast Bread dough
(see page 144 and below)*

For the topping

½ quantity Tomato Sauce (see page 66)

8oz (250g) low-fat mozzarella, grated

*about 4oz (125g) garlic cloves,
pan-braised (see page 78)*

8 plum tomatoes, sliced

handful of fresh basil leaves, chopped

1 Prepare the dough up to step 7 of Basic Yeast Bread and divide into 2 or 4 compact balls. Lightly flour a work surface, then roll the dough into circles, rolling from the center out to the edges, turning at intervals. Put the disks on lightly floured baking sheets.

2 Spread Tomato Sauce over each disk, leaving a 1in (2.5cm) border all around. Add the mozzarella, garlic cloves, and tomatoes evenly over the sauce.

3 Bake in a preheated oven for 15–25 minutes, until the filling is bubbly and the edges of the dough are puffed and golden. Garnish the pizzas with the fresh basil.

OTHER TOPPINGS

Peppers & Feta Cheese (see page 12): replace the mozzarella with crumbled low-fat feta cheese. Top with ½ quantity Silky Stir-Fried Sweet Pepper Strips (see page 71), 2 or 3 chopped black olives, and sprigs of thyme.

Sausage & Creamy Spinach (see page 12): replace the mozzarella with ricotta. Scatter small meatballs made from ½ quantity Spicy Citrus-Scented Mexican Sausages (see page 94). Top with cooked fresh spinach and broiled eggplant slices.

Tomato & Red Onion (see page 12): spread the Tomato Sauce and ½ quantity Cherry Tomato & Red Onion Salsa (see page 61), scatter zucchini and eggplant slices, and top with shavings of Parmesan.

Mushroom & Pesto (see page 12): spread the Tomato Sauce and top with ½ quantities of Mushrooms Made Wild (see page 74) and White Pesto (see page 63), a few strips of well-trimmed prosciutto, and 1 or 2 black olives, slivered off their pits.

VARIATIONS

Filled Pizza: divide the dough into 2 balls, then roll them into circles. Spread any pizza topping over one of the circles, lay the other one on top, and pinch the edges together to seal. Bake for 15–20 minutes.

Filled Calzone: divide the dough into 4 or 8 balls and roll out into circles. Lightly puree together 1lb (500g) each ricotta and lightly cooked spinach and spread over the circles. Add 4oz (125g) shredded low-fat mozzarella, a few slices of well-trimmed prosciutto cut into strips, and season to taste. Fold over and pinch the ends to seal. Bake for 15 minutes for small calzone, 25 minutes for larger ones.

Filled Rolls: prepare the dough as for calzone (above), then spread the calzone filling or any pizza topping. Roll into cylinders and pinch the ends closed. Leave in a warm place to rise for 20 minutes before baking, following the timings for calzone.

 Per serving

Total fat (g)	10
Saturated fat (g)	5
Unsaturated fat (g)	5
Cholesterol (mg)	19
Sodium (mg)	713
Calories	700

 Oven temperature
400°F/200°C

 Baking time
15–25 minutes

 Makes
4 servings, either as
4 8in (20cm) pizzas, or
2 12in (30cm) pizzas

PEPPERS & FETA
CHEESE PIZZA

TOMATO &
MOZZARELLA
PIZZA

WILD MUSHROOM BREAD

This loaf is best eaten a day after baking. If you do not have a food processor, the dough can be easily mixed in a large bowl. It takes a little longer to mix and knead, but the result is just as successful.

INGREDIENTS

2oz (60g) dried porcini

1¼ cups (400ml) very warm water

½oz (15g) cake yeast

¼ cup (125g) instant, unseasoned potato flakes

4–5 cups (500g) unbleached flour, plus extra to dust

1 tsp sea salt

1 Soak the porcini in the water for 20–30 minutes. Drain and reserve the liquid. Rinse the porcini under cold running water and chop finely. Strain the soaking water through a coffee filter or several thicknesses of paper towels. Set aside the liquid and the porcini.

2 Mix the yeast with ½ cup (150ml) of the soaking liquid. Stir to dissolve the yeast.

3 Put the potato flakes, 4 cups of flour, and salt in a food processor. Stir the remaining soaking liquid into the yeast mixture. Turn on the processor and pour the yeast mixture gradually through the feed tube. Stop occasionally to scrape the mixture from the sides of the bowl so the ingredients are well mixed. If the dough is too wet, add more

flour. When the mixture has formed a cohesive dough, add the porcini pieces and process briefly.

4 Put the dough on a very lightly floured work surface. Knead rhythmically for 5–10 minutes, until smooth and springy. If it is sticky and difficult to handle, dust with a little flour, but bear in mind the dough should be a little sticky (too much flour will make the loaf heavy). Press the dough with your finger – if the indentation springs back, it is ready.

5 Form the dough into a smooth ball, put it in a large, lightly floured bowl, and lightly dust the top with flour. Cover loosely with plastic wrap. Place a roasting pan filled with boiling water on the oven floor. Put the bowl of dough in the oven and let rise for 1½ hours, until doubled in size.

6 Punch down the dough with floured knuckles and knead it very briefly. Let it rest while you lightly flour a nonstick baking sheet. Remove the pan of water from the oven; preheat the oven.

7 Form the dough into a plump, round loaf and put it on the baking sheet. Cover with plastic wrap and leave in a warm place for 30–45 minutes to double in size.

8 Fill the pan with boiling water and place it on the oven floor. Put the dough in the preheated oven and bake for 40–55 minutes. Spray it with water occasionally during baking. For the last few minutes, turn the loaf upside down and set it directly on the oven shelf. The bread is done when it is golden brown and sounds hollow when the bottom is tapped with the knuckles. Let the loaf cool (this improves its flavor).

Per recipe quantity

Total fat (g)	8
Saturated fat (g)	1
Unsaturated fat (g)	5
Cholesterol (mg)	0
Sodium (mg)	2942
Calories	2290

 Oven temperature
400°F/200°C

 Baking time
40–55 minutes

 Makes
one 9–10in (23–25cm) round loaf

BANANA CHOCOLATE LOAF

This cake has been very well tested, since my family and friends adore it. The only fat comes from the grated chocolate, yet the cake tastes quite rich. Serve it as it is or spread slices with Chestnut Chocolate Cream (see page 120).

INGREDIENTS

2 very ripe bananas (they should be black!)

1 cup (250ml) orange juice

2½ cups (300g) self-rising flour

1 tsp baking powder

pinch of salt

1oz (30g) semisweet chocolate, grated

2 egg whites

⅔ cup (150g) light brown sugar

1 Line a 9 x 5¾ x 2¾in (1kg) loaf pan with waxed paper and spray with oil-water spray.

2 Mash the bananas and orange juice together, blending well.

3 Sift together the flour, baking powder, and salt. Add the chocolate and stir into the banana mixture. Whisk for 1–2 minutes.

4 Whisk the egg whites until stiff, then gradually add the sugar, whisking well after each addition. Fold the egg whites into the flour mixture until evenly mixed. Spoon the mixture into the pan and smooth the top. Bake in a preheated oven for about 1 hour.

5 When the loaf has risen and is golden brown, check that it is ready by inserting a cake tester or skewer into the center. When it comes out clean, the loaf is done.

6 Cool in the pan on a wire rack for a few minutes. Loosen the loaf carefully all around the inside of the pan and turn out. Peel off the waxed paper.

7 Cool thoroughly, then store, wrapped in foil, in an airtight container. It is best eaten on the day after it is made.

 Per slice

Total fat (g)	1
Saturated fat (g)	<1
Unsaturated fat (g)	<1
Cholesterol (mg)	neg
Sodium (mg)	165
Calories	174

 Oven temperature
325°F/160°C

Baking time
1 hour–1 hour 10 minutes

Makes
12 slices

CARROT CRANBERRY LOAF

My version of carrot cake is rich with fruit but has no fat at all, not even an egg yolk. Classic carrot cake is iced with a cream cheese frosting. Spread slices of this luscious loaf with one of the Ricotta Cream Toppings (see page 137) instead.

INGREDIENTS

1 medium Granny Smith or other tart eating apple, peeled, cored, and diced

⅖lb (180g) carrots, finely grated

1 cup (250g) golden raisins, soaked overnight in 1 cup (250ml) cranberry juice

2½ cups (300g) self-rising flour

1 tsp baking powder

pinch of salt

1 pinch of ground cinnamon

3 tsp ground mixed spice

2 egg whites, lightly beaten

⅔ cup (165g) light brown sugar

1 Line a 9 x 5¾ x 2¾in (1kg) nonstick loaf pan with waxed paper. Spray with oil-water spray.

Put the apple, carrot, raisins, and juice in a saucepan. Bring to a boil and set aside to cool. In a separate bowl, sift together the flour, baking powder, salt, and spices.

2 Whisk the egg whites until stiff, then gradually whisk in the sugar, making a stiff meringue.

3 Add the fruit mixture to the flour, beating well for 1–2 minutes. Fold in the meringue. Turn the mixture into the prepared pan and smooth the top. Bake in a preheated oven for 1½–1¾ hours, or until the loaf has risen and is golden brown.

4 Cool the cake on a wire rack, then turn it out and remove the paper. Store wrapped in foil.

 Per slice

Total fat (g)	<1
Saturated fat (g)	neg
Unsaturated fat (g)	<1
Cholesterol (mg)	0
Sodium (mg)	154
Calories	223

 Oven temperature
325°F/160°C

 Baking time
1½–1¾ hours

 Makes
12 slices

ANISE & FIG POLENTA CAKE

Another no-fat gem, based on a high-fat Italian classic. I love the combined flavors of anise (from fennel seeds, in this recipe) and fig in this gorgeously moist cake. Serve it in slices with Sweet Vermouth Syrup (see page 129).

INGREDIENTS

2 cups (550ml) water

2 pinches of salt

1 tsp vanilla extract

1 cup (180g) coarse yellow cornmeal

6 egg whites

pinch of cream of tartar

⅔ cup (150g) superfine sugar

⅓ cup (75g) golden raisins

½ cup (150g) dried figs, diced

1–1½ tbsp fennel seeds

1¼ cups (150g) self-rising flour, sifted with 1 tsp baking powder

1 Bring the water to just below a boil in a pan. Add the salt and vanilla. Pour in the cornmeal in an even stream, whisking well. With a wooden spoon, stir and cook until the mixture is smooth, thick, and pulls away from the pan's side.

2 Whisk the egg whites and cream of tartar to soft peaks.

Whisk in the sugar, a little at a time, until the eggs are glossy and hold firm peaks.

3 Add the golden raisins, figs, and fennel seeds to the cornmeal, beating until well blended. Then add half the egg white mixture, with the flour and baking powder. Stir until well blended. Fold in the remaining egg white mixture until well incorporated.

4 Lightly oil-water spray a 8 x 2in (20 x 5cm) nonstick, loose-bottomed cake pan and spoon the mixture into it.

5 Bake in a preheated oven for about 50–55 minutes, until the top is dry and slightly crackled, and a cake tester inserted into the middle comes out clean.

6 Loosen the sides of the cake with a narrow spatula and remove from the pan. Let cool on a wire rack.

 Per slice

Total fat (g)	1
Saturated fat (g)	neg
Unsaturated fat (g)	1
Cholesterol (mg)	0
Sodium (mg)	140
Calories	194

 Oven temperature
350°F/180°C

Baking time
50–55 minutes

Makes
12 slices

ALMOND COOKIES

These cookies are designed to be served with sorbets, ice cream, or cheesecake mousses. Best is to cut them in half, then set them into the dessert at a jaunty angle.

INGREDIENTS

2½oz (75g) amaretti cookies

1 cup (75g) Grape-Nuts® cereal

2 egg whites

1 Put the cookies and cereal into a blender or food processor and process to coarse crumbs.

2 Lightly beat the egg whites and mix with the dry mixture until thoroughly combined.

3 Lightly spray a nonstick baking sheet with oil-water spray. Spoon tablespoons of the crumb mixture onto the baking

sheet, leaving spaces between the heaps. Flatten gently with the back of a spoon.

4 Transfer to a preheated oven and bake for 7–10 minutes, then put the baking sheet on a wire rack to cool.

5 When the cookies are cool, loosen them with a narrow spatula and lift them off the baking sheet. Store the cold cookies in an airtight container until needed.

 Per biscuit

Total fat (g)	neg
Saturated fat (g)	0
Unsaturated fat (g)	neg
Cholesterol (mg)	0
Sodium (mg)	39
Calories	30

 Oven temperature
350°F/180°C

 Baking time
7–10 minutes

 Makes
20 cookies

VANILLA MERINGUES

Meringues make perfect, tiny, crunchy, no-fat cookies. Serve these as they are with sorbets, ice creams, and mousses. Even better, sandwich smaller meringues together with a rich filling. Illustrated below are heaped teaspoon-size meringues sandwiched together with Chestnut Chocolate Cream (see page 120).

INGREDIENTS

3 egg whites, at room temperature

pinch of cream of tartar

pinch of salt

½ cup (150g) superfine sugar

1 tsp natural vanilla extract

1 Beat the egg whites, cream of tartar, and salt until foamy. Still beating briskly, add the sugar 1–2 tablespoons at a time, until shiny and stiff and the mixture holds firm peaks. Fold in the vanilla.

2 Line two baking sheets with nonstick baking parchment. Drop the mixture, in teaspoonfuls or tablespoonfuls, depending on the size you want, on the sheets, leaving 1in (2.5cm) around each one. Bake in a preheated oven for 45–60 minutes.

3 Turn the oven off. Leave the meringues in the oven for at least 3 hours, or overnight. Do not open the oven until the time is up. Store meringues in an airtight container until ready to serve.

 Per recipe quantity

Total fat (g)	0
Saturated fat (g)	0
Unsaturated fat (g)	0
Cholesterol (mg)	0
Sodium (mg)	365
Calories	625

Oven temperature
225°F/110°C

Baking time
45–60 minutes

Makes
40 teaspoon-size meringues (20 pairs)

BREAKFASTS

BREAKFAST IS A LOVELY MEAL: what better way to start the day than with glorious food? On busy days there may be little time for anything but a toasted ricotta-spread bagel, or a quick bowl of cereal and fruit, but on weekends, when breakfast often becomes brunch, it's time to pull out all the stops. It is now believed that the occasional whole egg won't hurt, but eggs are not the be-all and end-all of breakfast. Try variations of oven-baked french toast – I give two fruit-filled recipes here – satisfyingly substantial savory clafoutis, with vegetables, or smoked haddock with crisp potatoes. What luxury!

ALMOST CLASSIC OMELET
cuts down on the egg yolks but does not omit them altogether.

OMELET FILLINGS

An imaginative filling turns a simple omelet into a feast. The one pictured (left) is filled with slivers of well-trimmed prosciutto, fresh tomato, and herbs. Other filling choices include many of the sauce, salsa, and vegetable recipes in this book. Suggested, right, are Mushrooms Made Wild (see page 74), Glazed Fennel, and Sweet & Sour Red Onions (see page 70).

MUSHROOMS MADE WILD

GLAZED FENNEL

SWEET & SOUR RED ONIONS

ALMOST CLASSIC OMELET

An all-egg white omelet is a daunting object. But, reduce the yolks and your omelet will be pale, but delicious.

INGREDIENTS

4 egg whites

2 whole eggs

salt and freshly ground black pepper

1–2 tsp chopped fresh herbs, optional

oil-water spray (see page 29)

about ½ cup (125ml) filling (see Omelet Fillings, above)

1 tbsp grated Parmesan, optional

1 Put the egg whites and whole eggs into a bowl. Add a little salt (not too much, or the egg protein toughens), pepper, and the herbs, if desired. Beat the eggs with a fork until well blended, 35–40 strokes. Do not overbeat or the mixture will be too thin. Lift your fork out of the mixture: when properly beaten, the egg will flow freely through the tines.

2 Spritz a nonstick skillet with oil-water spray and warm it over medium-high heat. When sizzling, with little beads of oil skittering around the pan, pour in the egg mixture.

3 Allow the eggs to set for 2–3 seconds. Then, using a wooden or nylon spatula, quickly but gently push the eggs toward the center of the pan. Work all around the perimeter of the pan, so the eggs form large, soft, moist curds.

4 Shake the pan rapidly, using sharp, definite movements, so the omelet forms an oval of fluffy, softly scrambled eggs in an envelope of coagulated egg.

5 In 10–15 seconds, when the omelet is set and cooked but still creamy and soft in the center, and not at all browned on the bottom, spoon the chosen filling down the center and sprinkle with grated cheese, if desired.

6 Slide the omelet onto a warm plate tilted against the pan. Let the omelet fold close over the filling as it slides off the pan. The whole operation should have taken less than a minute. Serve at once.

VARIATION

Frittata: first preheat the broiler. Prepare the omelet through step 5, above. Put the skillet under the hot broiler to set the omelet top and melt the cheese, if using. Slide the frittata onto a plate, broiled side up. Cut into wedges to serve.

 Per serving (no filling)

Total fat (g)	6
Saturated fat (g)	2
Unsaturated fat (g)	4
Cholesterol (mg)	193
Sodium (mg)	184
Calories	97

 Makes
2 servings

MUSHROOM CLAFOUTI

Sweet clafouti is a French classic (see page 131). Savory versions make festive and substantial breakfast or brunch dishes. A clafouti puffs up dramatically, like a soufflé, and is wonderful served hot or warm.

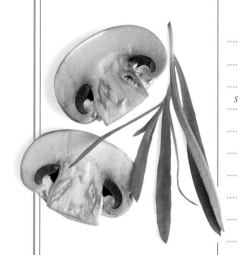

INGREDIENTS

For the filling

5oz (150g) mushrooms, quartered

½oz (15g) dried porcini

2 sun-dried tomatoes, chopped

2 olives, slivered off their pits

1¼ cups (300ml) stock (see page 30)

½ cup (125ml) dry white wine

several dashes of teriyaki and Worcestershire sauces

For the batter

¾ cup (105g) all-purpose flour

salt and freshly ground black pepper

1¼ cups (300ml) skim milk

3 tbsp skim milk powder

6 tbsp low-fat plain yogurt

1 whole egg

3 egg whites

2 tsp spicy mustard

several dashes of Tabasco sauce

2 tbsp each chopped fresh thyme and tarragon

1 tbsp grated Gruyère

2 tbsp grated Parmesan

1 For the filling, put all the ingredients in a skillet. Bring to a boil over medium-high heat and simmer briskly until the liquid has almost evaporated.

2 For the batter, put the flour in a bowl and season. Whisk together the remaining ingredients except the cheeses. Pour into the flour and stir until just mixed with no lumps. Do not overmix.

3 Oil-water spray a 10in (25cm) nonstick tart pan. Pour in the batter. Scatter the filling, leaving a 1in (2.5cm) border all around, and sprinkle with the cheeses. Bake in a preheated oven for 30–40 minutes, until set, lightly browned, and puffed. Cool on a wire rack.

 Per serving

Total fat (g)	4
Saturated fat (g)	2
Unsaturated fat (g)	2
Cholesterol (mg)	42
Sodium (mg)	304
Calories	179

 Oven temperature
375°F/190°C

 Baking time
30–40 minutes

 Makes
6 servings

RED ONION CLAFOUTI

Clafouti is delicious when cooled, and this red onion version would fare particularly well at a picnic.

INGREDIENTS

For the filling

2 large red onions, halved and sliced into crescents

about 1¼ cups (300ml) stock (see page 30)

about ½ cup (125ml) red wine

For the batter

1¼ cups (300ml) skim milk

3 tbsp skim milk powder

6 tbsp low-fat plain yogurt

3 egg whites

1 whole egg

¾ cup (105g) all-purpose flour

2–3 tbsp grated Parmesan

1 Boil the onions, stock, and wine in a covered nonstick pan for 3–5 minutes. Uncover and simmer until the onions are tender. Stir in a little wine and stock to loosen any browned bits. Oil-water spray a 10in (25cm) nonstick tart pan.

2 For the batter, whisk together all the ingredients except the flour and cheese. Put the flour in a bowl and stir in the liquid until just mixed with no lumps.

3 Pour the batter into the pan. Scatter the filling, leaving a 1in (2.5cm) border all around, then sprinkle on the cheese. Bake in a preheated oven for 30–40 minutes until set, browned, and puffed.

 Per serving

Total fat (g)	3
Saturated fat (g)	2
Unsaturated fat (g)	1
Cholesterol (mg)	39
Sodium (mg)	209
Calories	167

 Oven temperature
375°F/190°C

 Baking time
30–40 minutes

 Makes
6 servings

SMOKED HADDOCK ON A NEST OF POTATOES

I love the contrast of the smoked, flaky fish against its crisp potato bed. This would make an elegant weekend breakfast or brunch.

INGREDIENTS

½lb (250g) potatoes, scrubbed but unpeeled

2 pinches of paprika

oil-water spray (see page 29)

salt and freshly ground black pepper

2 pieces of smoked haddock, each about 5oz (150g), skinned and bones removed with tweezers

bunch of watercress, to garnish

1 Slice the potatoes paper-thin: using the slicer on the side of a grater is the best way to get fine slices. Put into a colander and rinse well, then drain and dry in a dish towel. Toss the slices with a pinch of the paprika and a spritz of oil-water spray.

2 Spray a baking sheet and spread the slices out. Bake in a preheated oven for 10 minutes, then stir them, spread out again, and bake for about 5 minutes more, until tender and lightly browned. They should be crisp in patches.

3 Sprinkle a pinch of paprika and a grinding of pepper over the fish. Lightly salt the potatoes and arrange in two piles on the baking sheet. Place a piece of fish over each pile of potatoes.

4 Bake for about 7 minutes, until just done. Garnish with watercress and serve with sautéed mushrooms alongside, if desired. (To sauté mushrooms, see The Morning "Fry-up," page 154.)

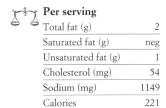

Per serving

Total fat (g)	2
Saturated fat (g)	neg
Unsaturated fat (g)	1
Cholesterol (mg)	54
Sodium (mg)	1149
Calories	221

Oven temperature
475°F/240°C

Baking time
22 minutes

Makes
2 servings

THE MORNING "FRY-UP"

There is something compelling about a huge fried breakfast: platters of mouth-watering food, ending the long fast of the night, and stoking the mind and body for the rigors of a new day. But now it's time to indulge in the ultimate postmodern "fry" – all the glory with little of the fat.

INGREDIENTS

4 poached eggs

4oz (125g) button mushrooms, pan-"fried" (see method)

4 tomatoes, halved, sprayed with oil-water spray and broiled

4 toasted slices of Wild Mushroom Bread (see page 146), with fruit preserve

Spicy Lima Beans (see page 114)

Breakfast Sausage Patties (see method)

1 Sauté the mushrooms in ⅓ cup (90ml) stock, a splash of dry sherry, and a dash of teriyaki sauce (see Techniques, page 30).

2 To make the Breakfast Sausage Patties, follow the recipe for Piquant Lemon Herb Meatballs (see page 95), but substitute half the amount of fresh sage for the mint, a whisper of nutmeg for the spices, and omit the Tabasco unless you crave fire early in the morning.

VARIATION

Postmodern Tex-Mex Breakfast: instead of toasted Wild Mushroom Bread and fruit preserves, serve a stack of warm tortillas. Serve the Spicy Lima Beans and leave the seasonings of the Piquant Lemon Herb Meatballs just as they are in the original recipe.

Per serving

Total fat (g)	13
Saturated fat (g)	4
Unsaturated fat (g)	8
Cholesterol (mg)	268
Sodium (mg)	1576
Calories	474

Makes
4 servings

SPOONBREAD CORN MUFFINS

These cornmeal muffins are virtually no-fat. Tender and light-as-a-feather, they rise to towering heights and are quite wonderful for breakfast.

INGREDIENTS

1¼ cups (165g) cornmeal, divided in half

1 cup (140g) all-purpose flour

½ tsp salt

½ tsp baking soda

2 tbsp mild honey

1 cup plus 2 tbsp (275ml) low-fat buttermilk

3 egg whites, beaten until foamy

1 cup (250ml) water

1 tsp vanilla extract

2 egg whites, beaten to stiff peaks

1 Sift half the cornmeal with the flour, salt, and baking soda. Stir the honey and buttermilk into the 3 egg whites.

2 Bring the water to a boil in a nonstick saucepan. Pour the remaining cornmeal into the water, whisking continuously. Take a wooden spoon and stir until the mixture is very smooth and pulls away from the sides of the pan (this happens very quickly). Scrape the mixture into a large bowl.

3 Alternate adding the egg white-buttermilk mixture and the sifted flour mixture into the cooked cornmeal. Stir in the vanilla. Whisk 2 spoonfuls of the 2 stiffly beaten egg whites in to lighten the mixture, then fold in the rest. Do not overmix.

4 Divide the batter among 12 paper muffin cups in a nonstick muffin tin. Bake in a preheated oven for 25–35 minutes, until well risen, lightly browned, and firm but springy when pressed. A cake tester inserted into the center should come out clean.

5 Cool the muffins, still in their paper cups but out of the pan, on a wire rack.

Per muffin

Total fat (g)	<1
Saturated fat (g)	neg
Unsaturated fat (g)	<1
Cholesterol (mg)	1
Sodium (mg)	125
Calories	111

Oven temperature
375°F/190°C

Baking time
25–35 minutes

Makes
12

CINNAMON BLUEBERRY FRENCH TOAST

This is a good recipe to prepare the night before. Make it up to the ready-for-the-oven stage and put it in the refrigerator. The next morning, bring it back to room temperature while the oven preheats.

INGREDIENTS

8–10 slices (about 6oz/180g) day-old baguette, sliced ¼in (5mm) thick

2 tbsp dried blueberries

2 tbsp raisins

2 whole eggs

2 egg whites

2 tbsp orange marmalade

2 cups (500ml) skim milk

2 tbsp skim milk powder

½ tsp ground cinnamon

2 tbsp granulated brown sugar

1 Arrange the slices of baguette in overlapping rows to cover the bottom of a baking dish. Scatter the blueberries and raisins evenly over the bread.

2 Beat the eggs and egg whites with the marmalade. Beat together the milk and milk powder and then beat them into the eggs with the cinnamon. Pour the mixture over the bread and, using a broad spatula, push the bread into the liquid.

3 Place the baking dish in a larger dish and pour boiling water in the larger dish to come halfway up the sides.

4 Bake in a preheated oven for 35–45 minutes, until puffed, set, and browned on top. Sprinkle with the brown sugar and serve the toast warm.

 Per serving

Total fat (g)	3
Saturated fat (g)	1
Unsaturated fat (g)	2
Cholesterol (mg)	66
Sodium (mg)	315
Calories	212

 Oven temperature
350°F/180°C

 Baking time
35–45 minutes

Makes
6 servings

OVEN-BAKED FRENCH TOAST WITH PEACHES

Ring the changes on this recipe with any fruit that you like. When peaches or nectarines are out of season, apples or pears work well.

INGREDIENTS

1½lb (750g) fresh peach wedges, peeled, or nectarine wedges, unpeeled

1 tbsp Cointreau

1 tsp vanilla extract

¼ cup (60ml) orange juice

6oz (180g) excellent quality day-old bread, sliced

1 whole egg

2 egg whites

2–3 tbsp peach or apricot sugar-free preserves

1 cup (250ml) skim milk

2 tbsp skim milk powder

1 Mix the fruit with the Cointreau, vanilla, and orange juice, then set aside.

2 Arrange the bread slices on the bottom of a tart dish, cutting them into halves or quarters, as necessary. Pour the peaches and their juice evenly over the bread. Set aside for a few minutes to allow the juices to soak into the bread.

3 Beat the whole egg and egg whites with the preserves. Beat the milk and milk powder together and then beat into the egg mixture to make a custard. Pour it evenly over the bread and fruit, using a spatula to press the bread into the custard.

4 Put the tart dish in a larger dish and fill the larger one with boiling water to come halfway up the sides.

5 Bake in a preheated oven for 35–45 minutes, until puffed and set. Serve warm.

 Per serving

Total fat (g)	2
Saturated fat (g)	neg
Unsaturated fat (g)	1
Cholesterol (mg)	33
Sodium (mg)	218
Calories	173

 Oven temperature
350°F/180°C

 Baking time
35–45 minutes

 Makes
6 servings

MENU IDEAS

METICULOUS MENU PLANNING, USING A CALCULATOR AND A TABLE OF FAT AND CALORIE VALUES, IS A PLEASURE-DEADENING AFFAIR. IF YOU PRACTICE LOW-FAT KITCHEN TECHNIQUES AND CENTER YOUR MEALS AROUND PLENTY OF VEGETABLES AND FRUITS, SUCH CALCULATIONS ARE UNNECESSARY. FILL YOUR MEALS WITH COLOR, TEXTURE, AND FLAVOR, CELEBRATE THE SEASONS, FEAST DAYS, HOLIDAYS, AND FRIENDSHIP, AND ENJOY FOOD FOR THE LIFE-GIVING ADVENTURE IT IS.

AUTUMN CELEBRATION

Smoky chicken; caramelized sweetness of roasted squash; apples and cranberries: pure autumn!

BASIC YEAST BREAD *page 144, with* SWEET POTATO SPREAD *page 51 and* BUTTERNUT SQUASH, GINGER & LIME PUREE
page 50

....

SMOKED ROSEMARY-LEMON CORNISH HENS
page 85

ORANGE-THYME SCENTED WILD RICE
page 115

....

APPLE & RAISIN CLAFOUTIS
page 131

FEASTS

ITALIAN VEGETARIAN FEAST

The fragrance of fennel and spices, fresh peaches and basil, wild mushrooms and balsamic: memorable.

FRAGRANT VEGETABLE SOUP
page 47

....

EGGPLANT & TOMATO GRATIN
page 79

TOMATO, PEACH & GRILLED PEPPER SALAD
page 58

WILD MUSHROOM BREAD
page 146

....

STRAWBERRIES IN LEMON BALSAMIC SYRUP
page 128

Below: Fragrant Vegetable Soup

& CELEBRATIONS

SUMMER CELEBRATION

Chili- and lime-infused chicken with a celebration of vegetables, herbs, and fruit: splendidly simple.

ROASTED VEGETABLE SALSA *page 65, with*
PITA CRISPS
page 53

....

BRAISED CHICKEN MEXICAN
page 87

COUSCOUS VEGETABLE SALAD
page 58

....

SWEET VERMOUTH-BATHED SUMMER PUDDING
page 126

Below: Sweet Vermouth-Bathed Summer Pudding

MEXICAN FIESTA

New World flavors and textures: corn, chili, roasted peppers, overflowing tortillas, dark chocolate: exhilarating.

CREAMY CORN DIP *page 52 and*
POTATO SKIN DIPPERS
page 53

....

SMOKED DUCK FAJITAS
page 90

....

CHOCOLATE SORBET
page 140

Above: Smoked Duck Fajitas

SPECIAL

FESTIVE SUNDAY BRUNCH

An elegant brunch begins with obligatory bagels (no bagels, no brunch!) and combines gorgeous textures, colors, and flavors.

BAGELS *with* HERBED RAITA *page 52*
and SLICED TOMATOES

SMOKED HADDOCK ON A NEST OF POTATOES
WITH SAUTEED MUSHROOMS
page 153
SILKY STIR-FRIED SWEET PEPPER STRIPS
page 71

CARAMELIZED PEARS *page 129, with* YOGURT
"WHIPPED CREAM"
page 137

Below: Smoked Haddock on a Nest of Potatoes

VEGETARIAN BIRTHDAY BASH

Cassata makes a rich, lavish birthday cake. The ravioli and the soup bring complexity and delicacy.

WHITE BEAN, SWEET
POTATO & FENNEL SOUP
page 49

GRILLED EGGPLANT & ZUCCHINI
page 81

OPEN RAVIOLI WITH TWO SAUCES
page 108

SALAD OF MIXED GREENS, TOMATOES,
AND HERBS

CASSATA
page 143

Above: Open Ravioli with Two Sauces

OCCASIONS

BIRTHDAY BASH

Herby artichokes, salmon with a blazing sauce, fragrant salsa, asparagus, blueberries: sheer luxury.

STUFFED ARTICHOKE HEARTS
page 76

....

SALMON WITH YELLOW PEPPER &
TARRAGON SAUCE *page 104*

MANGO & FENNEL SALSA *page 61 and*
STEAMED ASPARAGUS *page 78*

SAUTE POTATOES WITH LEMON & MINT
page 73

....

ANGEL CAKE *page 143, with* BLUEBERRY
COMPOTE *page 130*

*Below: Salmon with Yellow Pepper
& Tarragon Sauce*

LOW-FAT CHRISTMAS DINNER

Christmas Day need not end in overconsumption and exhaustion. Try an enlightened feast instead.

SPICY SWEET POTATO BISQUE *page 48*

WILD MUSHROOM PATE *page 51, with* PITA CRISPS
page 53

....

DUCK BREASTS WITH CRANBERRY CHUTNEY *page 89*

SPICED GREEN BEANS WITH LIME *page 81*

GARLIC & LEMON-ROASTED POTATOES *page 74*

....

RASPBERRY ALMOND CREAM TRIFLE *page 134*

CHOCOLATE DIPPED FRUITS *and* TRUFFLES
pages 122 and 123

Above: Chocolate Dipped Fruits and Truffles

EVERYDAY, BUT

Pasta Supper

Transcend spaghetti and meatballs! Family meals can shine with color and excitement.

PENNE *with* TOMATO, GARLIC &
PEPPER SAUCE
page 64

....

PIQUANT LEMON HERB MEATBALLS
page 95

ROASTED BEETS, ORANGE &
ARUGULA SALAD
page 56

....

MANGO SORBET
page 140

Below: Roasted Beets, Orange & Arugula Salad

Elegant Breakfast

An upscale and fancy variation on a traditional theme: eggs, sausages, mushrooms, and fruit.

ALMOST CLASSIC OMELET WITH
VEGETABLE FILLINGS
page 151

....

BREAKFAST SAUSAGE PATTIES
page 154

MUSHROOMS MADE WILD
page 74

....

MANGO MILLEFEUILLE
page 136

Above: Almost Classic Omelet

DIFFERENT

VEGETABLE SUPPER

Rosy-tinted cauliflower, crunchy, spicy fries, carrot-
and pepper-studded beans: heavenly color!

CANNELLINI BEAN & CHICKPEA SALAD
page 56

....

CAULIFLOWER STIR-FRIED IN RED WINE
page 69

SPICY OVEN FRIES
page 72

GLAZED FENNEL
page 70

....

FROZEN STRAWBERRY YOGURT
page 141

Below: Cauliflower Stir-Fried in Red Wine

POLENTA FEAST

Flavor-infused polenta, feisty sauce, pungent onions,
aromatic sausages: beautiful and satisfying.

GRILLED POLENTA SQUARES
page 112

ARRABIATTA SAUCE
page 66

SWEET & SOUR RED ONIONS
page 70

SPICY CITRUS-SCENTED MEXICAN
SAUSAGES
page 94

....

PEACH SALAD
page 128

Above: Grilled Polenta Squares

FAT FACTS

ALL FATS, WHETHER THEY ARE highly saturated animal fats, polyunsaturated or monounsaturated oils, margarines, or the fats or oils in nuts, avocados, or coconuts, provide 9 calories per gram (approximately 120 calories per tablespoon). These are calories that are stored and metabolized into body fat in an extremely quick and efficient fashion.

So-called "low-fat spreads" may contain less fat than butter or margarine because they have been diluted with something (water, air, or buttermilk, for example), but they still contain substantial amounts of health-threatening and calorie-dense fat. I have never understood the need for low-fat spreads. You can't really cook with them, because they are too watery. Their sole purpose seems to be to grease your bread or toast. Do you really want to add fat to your diet simply to ruin your toast and your beautiful bread?

SATURATED *VERSUS* UNSATURATED

The whole saturated-unsaturated (mono and poly) story can be incredibly confusing. To explain: it is the fatty acids in fat, defined by their chemical structures as saturated, monounsaturated, or polyunsaturated, that decide a fat's type. If a fat contains a higher proportion of saturated fatty acids than of polyunsaturated, it is defined as a saturated fat – and vice versa.

Saturated fats are found mostly in animal products, and most of them are solid at room temperature. **Monounsaturated fats** are found in olive and rapeseed oils and in fat spreads made from them. **Polyunsaturated fats,** often liquid at room temperature, are found in vegetable oils such as sunflower, safflower, and canola, and in cereals, nuts, and seeds.

While animal fats, including dairy fats (butter, cream, and whole-milk products), lard, and poultry drippings, contain a high percentage of saturated fatty acids, it is interesting to note that three vegetable oils – palm oil, palm kernel oil, and coconut oil – are even higher in saturates than butter.

So if a product is labeled "made with vegetable shortening only" or "contains vegetable fat," it does not automatically follow that the product is therefore high in unsaturates. Other vegetable oils are higher in monounsaturates and polyunsaturates, although they also contain some saturates.

Since a fat with a higher proportion of unsaturation is often liquid at room temperature, some solid margarines and solid vegetable shortening are manufactured by putting highly unsaturated vegetable oil through a hydrogenation process to firm it up, so that it will be, if not hard, then "spreadable."

This hydrogenation process actually causes the oil to become saturated; in fact, saturated in a way that produces trans-fatty acids – fatty acids that are not found naturally in food or in our bodies, and are suspected of causing even more health problems than naturally saturated fats.

In evaluating this information, just remember that all fat is equally fattening, whatever the makeup of its chemical bonds.

FATS AND HEALTHY EATING

While much solid scientific research reveals a connection between highly saturated fats and disease, especially (but not only) heart and artery disease, the unsaturated fats have also been implicated in disease, including several kinds of cancer. So, cutting back on highly saturated fats only, either for weight control or health, makes little sense. But eliminating added fats and high-fat foods makes perfect sense.

The human body needs a certain amount of dietary fat to function. But there is plenty of what you need in a bountiful diet of fish, lean meat and poultry, vegetables, fruits, and grains. And the masses of these foods (plus skim milk powder and the oil-water spray) used in the recipes in this book will give you a full complement of fat-soluble vitamins (important vitamins found in dietary fat) as well.

Epidemiological studies of the Inuit (Eskimos) of Greenland show that fish oil seems to be heart beneficial. The incidence of heart disease among these people, who eat a diet high in fish fat, is low. Fish fat may indeed be beneficial, and fish is rich in the fat-soluble vitamins as well. It's interesting that squid and shellfish, although not particularly fatty, contain a high proportion of Omega-3 fatty acids (the components of fish fat believed to be heart-healthy). So, unless you suffer from a medical problem that precludes the ingestion of any fat, a few fatty fish meals a week are wise choices. Even the fattiest fish are relatively low in calories.

WHAT ABOUT CHOLESTEROL?

Cholesterol is a fatty substance that is manufactured in the body and is important to the body's functioning. It is the excess cholesterol levels in the blood that concern medical researchers. On the scientific level, there is much controversy. Does dietary cholesterol – that is, the cholesterol in food – affect levels of blood cholesterol? Does it contribute to heart disease? And what about "good" cholesterol and "bad" cholesterol? Does olive oil (and other highly monounsaturated oils) really raise levels of "good" cholesterol, as has been claimed?

The truth is, there are no easy answers. The whole cholesterol story, on both a medical and a scientific level, is fraught with debate and conflicting theories. On a practical level, there is no need to be too concerned. If you have cut added fats and high-fat foods from your diet, you have done much toward reducing your total blood cholesterol levels and restoring the proper balance between so-called "good" (HDL or high-density lipoprotein) and "bad" (LDL or low-density lipoprotein) cholesterol.

It is now generally believed that it is the total fat intake that may have the effect of raising blood cholesterol levels, not just frequent consumption of high-cholesterol foods. It seems best to ignore current media exhortations to eat lashings of olive oil or canola oil or other highly monounsaturated oils to benefit your cholesterol levels. Olive oil and the others are all pure fat. Eliminate excess fat from your life, and you will be doing the best thing possible to reduce and rebalance your blood cholesterol levels.

INDEX

ACKNOWLEDGMENTS

Author's Appreciation
As always, my family has provided support, love, and a deep and abiding belief in my work (as I believe in theirs). Although we now live and work in separate places, the bond is as strong as ever. Thank you, Steve; thank you, Shawm. A big thank you to the Fairman clan for being such good neighbors, and to my young neighbors Joe and Thomas for keeping my life lively and intellectually stimulating. How pleasant it is to become reacquainted with dinosaurs. Warm thanks to Janice Murfitt for her calm competence, to Ian O'Leary for his brilliant camera work, and to Sandie Mitchel-King for her invaluable help with every facet of my work. I'm grateful to Marlena Spieler and Alan McLaughlan for their tasting input, and our far-ranging chats about food and life. I'm grateful as well to all my Roman Road chums. I wouldn't trade life on the Roman for any other place on earth! Hugs and kisses to Katie Ashley, my best Roman Road friend of all, who is always there for me, and to Janet Tod, whose work on canvas embodies all that I feel about food, pattern, and color. What a privilege it is to have such friends! And, finally, heartfelt and grateful thanks to Jeanette Hoare, Tonianne Kempson, and Brenda Huebler, who all, in their own way, help to keep chaos at bay. And Jeanette: you are such a pleasure to feed. May your enthusiasm never dim. The oven-baked Blueberry French Toast is especially dedicated to you.

Dorling Kindersley would like to thank Hannah Attwell for design assistance, Tracey Clarke for initial design work, Lorna Damms and Julia Pemberton Hellums for editorial assistance, Jasmine Challis for the nutritional analyses, Hilary Bird for the index, Oona van den Berg for home economy, Emma Brogli for photographic assistance, and Emma Murfitt for hand modeling.

DK Publishing, Inc., would like to thank Kathy Mackinnon for testing the baking recipes and Christy Nordstrom for testing the recipes with Quark for the US edition.

Picture Credits:
Photography by Ian O'Leary, except: Dave King 30 top; Patrick McLeavy 26–27, 28, 29, 30 bottom, 31 (except top), 32, 33, 34 (except top), 35 (except middle row, first two pictures), 36 (except top), 37, 126 top; David Murray 136 bottom; Clive Streeter 7, 9, 10–11, 14, 15, 21, 60, 82–3, 121, 135, 136 top.